PREACHING HOSEA, AMOS, & MICAH

PREACHING HOSEA, AMOS, & MICAH

CHARLES L. AARON JR.

ST. LOUIS, MISSOURI

Copyright ©2005 by Charles L. Aaron Jr.

First published in 2005 by Chalice Press.

All rights reserved. For permission to reuse content, please contact the author at CLA56@aol.com.

Bible quotations, unless otherwise noted, are from the *New Revised Standard Version Bible,* copyright 1989, Division of Christian Education of the National Council of the Churches of Christ in the United States of America. Used by permission. All rights reserved.

Scripture quotations marked (NIV) are taken from the HOLY BIBLE, NEW INTERNATIONAL VERSION®. NIV®. Copyright © 1973, 1978, 1984 by International Bible Society. Used by permission of Zondervan Publishing House. All rights reserved.

Those quotations marked RSV are from the *Revised Standard Version of the Bible,* copyright 1952, [2nd edition, 1971] by the Division of Christian Education of the National Council of the Churches of Christ in the United States of America. Used by permission. All rights reserved.

ISBN Print: 9781603500296

Published by Lucas Park Books
www.lucasparkbooks.com

This book is dedicated to three important mentors and friends:
Scott Black Johnston
Richard Lischer
W. Sibley Towner

Contents

Contributors	ix
Preface	x
Introduction: What Is a Prophetic Preacher?	1
1. Introduction to Hosea	12
2. Hosea 2:14–23	24
"A Second Honeymoon"*	28
"A Marriage Made in Heaven and Broken on Earth"	32
A. CARTER SHELLEY	
3. Hosea 11:1–11	39
"Will God Give Up on Us?"	44
"Hoping in the Love of God"	48
ANN I. HOCH	
4. Introduction to Amos	53
5. Amos 5:18–24	64
"Rain in the Forecast"	66
"Let Justice Roll"	71
WILLIAM C. TURNER	
6. Amos 7:10–17	78
"Priest or Prophet?"	80
"Showdown at Bethel"	84
VIRGIL P. HOWARD	

---

*The first sermon in each chapter is a sermon that the author has preached.

7. Introduction to Micah	92
8. Micah 4:1–7	101
"A Breath of Fresh Air"	102
"A Vision in Stained Glass"	107
David Schnasa Jacobsen	
9. Micah 5:1–5a	111
"A Strange Hope"	115
"Micah's Christmas Surprise"	118
Page L. D. Creach	
10. Micah 6:1–8	126
"God's Courtroom"	128
"The Minimum Daily Requirement"	132
Timothy K. Bruster	
"Check!"	139
Alyce M. McKenzie	
Notes	144

Contributors

Timothy K. Bruster is senior pastor of the First United Methodist Church in Fort Worth, Texas.

Page L. D. Creach is interim associate pastor for adult discipleship, Fox Chapel Presbyterian Church in Pittsburgh, Pennsylvania.

Ann I. Hoch is the vice president for advancement and church relations at the University of Dubuque.

Virgil P. Howard is professor of supervised ministry at Perkins School of Theology, Southern Methodist University.

David Schnasa Jacobsen is associate professor of homiletics at Waterloo Lutheran Seminary.

Alyce M. McKenzie is assistant professor of homiletics at Perkins School of Theology, Southern Methodist University.

A. Carter Shelley is a Presbyterian minister, researcher, and writer. She lives in Wilkesboro, North Carolina, and teaches part-time at Wake Forest Divinity School and Appalachian State University.

William C. Turner is a Baptist pastor and associate professor of the practice of homiletics at The Divinity School, Duke University.

Preface

We hear occasionally of people who go to a flea market, shop around, and buy a table that strikes their fancy. This table likely sat unnoticed by the other shoppers. The buyer takes the table home, polishes it up, and decides on a whim to have it appraised. During the appraisal, the buyer is astonished to find that the table, perhaps purchased for only a few dollars, is a valuable antique! With a discerning eye and a bit of effort, a real treasure is found in an unexpected place.

For pastors, reading the books of Hosea, Amos, and Micah can be similar to this experience. Preachers often pass these books by when shopping for a sermon text. At first glance, these books may appear too dusty and rough to be promising. All three of them sound angry and judgmental. They allude to political events that no longer matter. Their writings are encrusted with sexist assumptions and violent images.

Nevertheless, the preacher who keeps on walking to shop elsewhere is missing a real treasure. These prophets write with passion, power, and deep theological insight. They are able to look at seemingly good, religious people and institutions and discern the spiritual decay that others missed, or chose not to see. These prophets are able to tear down a facade of false piety, but then to build up a sturdy structure of faith founded on God's grace. Surely, such ancient treasures are worth the effort to polish them up for use in the contemporary pulpit.

To extend the metaphor, this book is about the care and treatment of ancient texts. Often, they are not ready for the pulpit in their raw form. The last thing we want to do with the prophets, however, is to sand off too many rough edges. If we strip off too much of their vivid language and shocking similes, we may leave the verve that makes them valuable on the workshop floor. What we want to polish off is the historical distance that masks their enduring message.

Preface xi

This book is for preachers. In examining these three prophetic writings and the selected preaching texts from them, I will concentrate on stimulating preachers' imaginations and on getting their creative juices flowing. I will spend only as much time and space on historical background and the editorial process behind the books as I need to. The commentaries cover those things, and this book is not intended to replace the commentaries or to enter too much into their important debates. I certainly will not ignore the contributions of the scholars. I will, however, spend most of my time and space discussing various ways to preach from these three prophets.

I will provide an introduction to each of the three books. Much of these introductions will cover parts of each book that are not included in the fuller treatment of the selected texts from that book. In these introductions I will make briefer suggestions for preaching from interesting texts from the three prophets.

From these three prophetic books, I have selected seven important texts: two from Hosea, two from Amos, and three from Micah. These seven truly represent the "classic" texts from these books. For each of these texts, I will provide a detailed exegesis and a discussion of the problems and possibilities in preaching from the text. Then, I will offer at least two sermons for each text. One of those sermons will be a sermon I preached in my ministry setting. The other sermon(s) will be from pastors and professors from the United States and Canada. It is my hope, and the hope of the other preachers who contributed to this volume, that these sermons will set the wheels in motion for your own sermon writing.

The sermons I have contributed to this volume were preached in two pastoral appointments in the North Texas Annual Conference of the United Methodist Church. These sermons have been field-tested in rural and small-town pastorates. From June 1998 until March 2000, I was pastor of the Holliday-Dundee charge in Archer County, Texas. From March 2000 until June 2003, I was pastor of the First United Methodist Church of Bowie, Texas.

The original audiences were salt-of-the-earth people facing the whole gamut of life's experiences. They deserve acknowledgment for their contribution to my whole ministry of preaching, and to this book. The sermon on Amos 7:10–17 was preached to my pastoral colleagues in the Wichita Falls District of the North Texas Annual Conference of the United Methodist Church. I thank them for their support and encourage-ment in the ministry. The sermon on Hosea 11 was also preached at the First United Methodist Church of Henrietta, Texas.

I want to thank the eight preachers who provided sermons for this volume. Their labors will be out of proportion to their reward. I would like to thank Dr. Kathryn Roberts, assistant professor of Old Testament at Austin Presbyterian Theological Seminary, who spent time in dialogue over this project with me. Further thanks go to Dr. John C. Holbert, Lois Craddock Perkins Professor of Preaching at Perkins School of Theology, who also engaged in dialogue over the book and read most of the manuscript, making many valuable suggestions.

Many people have supported my ministry and scholarship over the years. First and foremost has been my wife, Sandra. She has heard most of my sermons more than once, but still listens attentively. I have taught courses in preaching and biblical studies at four seminaries: Union/PSCE, Austin Presbyterian Theological Seminary, Duke University Divinity School, and Perkins School of Theology. I thank all four faculties for the opportunities.

INTRODUCTION

What Is a Prophetic Preacher?[1]

Several years ago, Ernest T. Campbell, then the pastor of Riverside Church in New York City, preached an "open letter" to Billy Graham.[2] In the sermon Campbell exhorted Graham to take a stand on several social issues, especially bombing in North Vietnam, but also on such issues as adequate housing, tax reform, racial discrimination, and others. In the sermon, Campbell himself explicitly called upon Graham to act as a prophet. He quoted a telegram sent by another prominent minister, Harry W. Andersen, which explicitly called Graham to act as a prophet.[3]

Dr. Graham did not respond directly to the open letter. Several weeks later he issued a statement in which he described himself as a "New Testament evangelist rather than an Old Testament prophet."

This incident from the 1970s raises the question of how contemporary clergy can carry on the ministry of the Old Testament prophets. We all likely would agree that the prophets are a valuable resource for preaching and ministry, but we have trouble knowing how to incorporate that resource into our ministry. How can contemporary pastors use the prophets as models for preaching and for the rest of our ministry?

Andersen and Campbell are correct that the prophets spoke out on controversial issues and that contemporary preachers ought not to ignore such issues, but we tend sometimes to limit the prophets to this aspect of ministry only. Graham is correct that pastors and other clergy have certain strengths on which they concentrate, but we tend sometimes to think the prophets

1

are a resource only for certain personality types or for pastors who specialize in social justice ministries.

We often think of well-known preachers, such as Martin Luther King Jr., Oscar Romero, William Sloane Coffin, or Gardner Taylor as "prophetic preachers." Often, such preachers enjoy national or international recognition. We usually assume that preachers who do not have an outspoken personality, a national audience, or a certain theological bent cannot appropriate the prophets in their ministry. We assume, along with Dr. Graham, that from among the choices of being prophets, pastors, evangelists, or priests, we must choose only one.

This book is written under the conviction that the prophets of the Old Testament, considered all together, were engaged in a comprehensive ministry that should serve as an example for every aspect of the contemporary pastor's vocation. The focus of this book, of course, is preaching. Here the ancient prophets give us an abundance of material to study and to emulate. Although some preachers are called "prophetic preachers" and seem more comfortable being outspoken, every pastor can learn from the Old Testament prophets.

Contemporary pastors may not be the exact equivalent of ancient Hebrew prophets, but we can incorporate their preaching and ministry into what we do in the modern-day church. The tendency to label our ministries (including our preaching) as "evangelistic," "teaching," "pastoral," or "doctrinal" is unfortunate. All ministry is comprehensive, just as the ministries of the ancient prophets were. We can draw inspiration from them and emulate them in all we do.

In seeking to draw upon the inspiration of the prophets, we are limited to the writings they left behind. We know very little about the lives of the prophets themselves. These articulate and intense speakers remain a mystery to us. Various attempts have been made to uncover the personalities behind the writings. Some have seen the prophets as ecstatic visionaries whose oracles were uttered from trancelike states. Others have seen the prophets as social reformers committed to certain political and economic agendas. Still others considered the prophets to be crystal ball gazers who could foretell the future. No single category adequately summarizes the work of the prophets. Their ministries were complex and far-reaching. They cannot be pigeonholed into one personality type, one style of ministry, or one theological emphasis.

The writings by and about the Old Testament prophets form a huge block of material, encompassing the Former Prophets (now known more commonly as the Deuteronomistic History), the Major Prophets, and the Minor Prophets. The Former Prophets, Joshua–2 Kings, are primarily historical narratives, but they contain many stories about prophets such as Nathan, Elijah, Elisha, Huldah, and others. These stories are a good source for our understanding of the ministry of the prophets in Israel and Judah.

The three Major Prophets (Isaiah, Jeremiah, and Ezekiel) and the twelve Minor Prophets (Hosea–Malachi) taken together constitute a massive collection of writings. It is shortsighted to assume that these voluminous books can easily be reduced to a few ideas or to one pattern of ministry. Deep engagement with the prophets reveals challenging and often astonishing insights for preaching and ministry.

The Prophets and Social Justice

Prophetic preaching! The very term brings to mind the bold proclamation of the prophets on social issues. Perhaps the image of the prophet as a courageous champion of social justice is rooted in the ministries of the eighth-century B.C.E. prophets. Isaiah, Hosea, Amos, and Micah delivered fiery, confrontational oracles to the leaders of Israel and Judah. They denounced economic stratification and the ill treatment of the poor and powerless. Typical of such oracles is Isaiah 1:17, "learn to do good, / seek justice, / rescue the oppressed, / defend the orphan, / plead for the widow." This sentence exhorts the leaders of Israel to take concrete action to protect the most vulnerable members of society. These actions were at the heart of the prophets' understanding of justice as a theological and ethical imperative.

The oracles that can reasonably be traced to the eighth-century prophets themselves contain a preponderance of this kind of preaching. They offer a theological critique of the problems of society. One function of a prophet is to diagnose the spiritual health of the community. In the eighth century, social and economic rifts marked Israelite society and revealed a spiritual sickness.[4]

We can admire the courage of the prophets and their attention to the poor and powerless, but we must admit that their rhetoric was often undiplomatic. Even though the prophets wrote in gripping and poetic language, they sometimes were downright insulting. Amos announced that YHWH did not accept the people's worship (5:21-23). Some of the prophets compared Israel and Judah to prostitutes (see, for example Hos. 1-3; Isa. 1:21; Ezek. 16). They threatened the people with God's anger and severe punishment, including total destruction of the kingdom itself (e.g., Amos 4:1-3, which contains the famous "cows of Bashan" remark).

Although powerful and dramatic language from the pulpit is admirable and in short supply, contemporary preachers must be careful when emulating the prophets' rhetoric. We have no mandate (at least in the United States) to threaten our congregations with military defeat. The real secret might be to capture the power and vividness of the prophets' rhetoric without sounding insulting or arrogant. Of course, some preachers may decide that such forceful and undiplomatic language is just what is needed in certain situations.

Despite that caveat, the theological and ethical substance of the prophets' call for justice has continuing significance for today. The prophets understood the great disparities in wealth between the rich and the poor in Israelite society as a sign of unfaithfulness to God. God has a right to expect Israel to form a just society, because of God's actions in forming and establishing Israel as a community. Amos spoke for God when he wrote, "Did I not bring Israel up from the land of Egypt?" (9:7). Because of God's mighty and gracious actions on behalf of Israel, the people had a responsibility to practice justice, understood as fairness in the court system, equitable distribution of goods and resources, and adequate protection for the vulnerable members of society.

That problems of justice with similarities to those of 8th century Israel exist in North America today is a proposition that hardly needs to be defended. The United States' business culture and tax system have created unconscionable concentrations of wealth in the hands of a few. Our court system, although it strives mightily to be fair, often produces unfair results. We may have a significant social safety net, but too many people fall through the tears in that net.

A ministry that emulates the ministry of the Old Testament prophets will interpret these social problems in the light of God's grace through Israel and of the Christ-event with its goal to redeem the creation. Preachers have a responsibility to minister to the needs of the poor and the disenfranchised, forthrightly calling attention to systemic issues of justice.

In this regard, the prophets offer a critique of the often highly individualized religious expression of the North American church. The individual and family problems of church members can be painful and difficult. They deserve the attention of the church, but the church must never forget that the prophets raise our sights to see larger issues of how society treats its most vulnerable members.

The role of the prophetic preacher is not necessarily to advocate for a particular political party or to champion any particular economic theory. The role of the prophetic preacher is to proclaim that because God has shown grace in creating us as a community, we have a responsibility to show justice to all members of society. The prophetic preacher is the persistent drumbeat, impossible to ignore, calling the church and society to seek justice. The prophetic preacher also preaches in hope, proclaiming that even if society's problems seem intractable, God is working to create and sustain justice.

The Prophets and Idolatry

The prophets may be known best for their advocacy of economic justice (at least in mainline denominations), but they were also concerned with the nation's idolatry. The prophets insisted on exclusive worship of and trusting dependence on YHWH alone. The people often failed in their exclusive devotion to YHWH.

The issue of idolatry in Israel is complex. Jeremiah accused the people of exchanging their gods (Jer. 2:11); Hosea ridiculed them for consulting a piece of wood (Hos. 4:12). The people of Israel did not consciously abandon worship of YHWH to practice another religion. They lived among neighbors who did not share their faith. This interaction led them to mingle elements of Baal worship (the religion of the Canaanites) with their own acts of worship.[5] Because Baal worship was oriented toward fertility, the people of Israel hoped that elements of Baal worship might ensure a good harvest.

During and after the exile, the people were tempted either to abandon worship of YHWH in despair, or assume that the Babylonian gods were superior to YHWH. The idolatry of the people resulted from carelessness and shortsightedness more than from the intentional rejection of their own faith.

The prophets often employed a two-fold strategy to combat idolatry. First, they used biting sarcasm to point out how ludicrous the making of stone, metal, or wooden idols was. (See for example Isa. 44:9–20.) Second, having debunked idols, the prophets affirmed the power, uniqueness, and reliability of YHWH (Isa. 44:21–28).

Contemporary idolatry is more subtle than Israel's prophets encountered. Some people currently practice blatant examples of idolatry, such as Tarot card readings and psychic hotlines. As silly as these seem to some of us, in some congregations, they may be a real problem. The sheer number of such services attests to their popularity and influence.

More often, idolatry takes the form of bad theology. The essence of idolatry is to worship a god in the hopes that the god will meet our needs without making demands on us. "Idolatry" is seeking concrete security, when our faith calls us to live with trust in God while recognizing our vulnerability. Churchgoers often expect God to bless and help them, without realizing that God calls them to lives of sacrifice and service. In essence, the church members often try to turn their own God into an idol.

I recently saw a cartoon about prayer. A man was looking into heaven with arms outstretched, saying, "Gimme, Gimme, Gimme." This perfectly exemplifies modern-day idolatry. The prophetic preacher will use a discerning eye to identify contemporary forms of idolatry, will use the pulpit to expose them, and will call the congregation to live in true faith. Such faith expects to serve, does not fear vulnerability, and trusts God unreservedly.

The Prophets and Pastoral Care

Preachers do not usually associate the Old Testament prophets with the pastoral care part of their ministries, even for the pastoral care done in preaching. We often think of the prophets as stem-winding preachers who confronted their congregations with oracles of judgment. We should remember that they also exercised the kind of compassion and restorative ministries we typically consider to be the realm of the pastor. We will point to two examples in the material about the Old Testament prophets that can serve as resources for ministry in times of grief and discouragement.

Second Kings 4:8–37 contains a touching story about the prophet Elisha's ministry to a Shunammite woman in grief. The Shunammite woman provided meals and lodging to Elisha in his travels. When he asks how he can repay her kindness, his assistant, Gehazi, points out that she has no son. In response to Elisha's promise of a son, the woman pleads, "No, my lord, O man of God; do not deceive your servant" (v. 16).

This first part of the story teaches about the grief of unfulfilled hopes. The woman had wanted to bear a child. She needed a son to take care of her if her aged husband were to die. Her remark to Elisha reveals the anguish of those who hope for what they likely will not receive. Her longing hurt so much that she would not allow herself to get her hopes up. People in comparable situations often exert tremendous psychic energy trying not to think about the thing for which they long.

Despite the woman's misgivings, Elisha's promise comes true: she bears a son. A few years later, however, tragedy strikes! The boy dies (from what sounds like an aneurysm). The woman's grief compels her to go to Elisha and Gehazi and to fall at the prophet's feet. Elisha miraculously revives the boy. This part of the story treats the grief of losing a loved one, in this case a child. One of the most difficult aspects of ministry is dealing with grief, especially when a child has died, or when a young child loses a parent. Elisha's compassion for the woman is a model for our ministry in grief.

This narrative relates the ministry of a prophet to a woman who experiences grief in two different ways. She experiences first the grief of longing for what may never happen. This is the grief of those who cannot have children, but it is also the grief of those whose career hopes fall short, whose health is chronically poor, who cannot obtain the education they wish for, or who long to marry but never have the opportunity. This kind of grief often goes unrecognized because people aren't aware of it. No one sends flowers or cards for this kind of grief. It can be a lonely experience.

The woman then experiences the grief of losing a child, a devastating experience. This is the grief of all parents who lose a child, of those who lose a spouse, of those who lose a job, and of those permanently injured in an accident. It is a sudden and shocking grief. Reflection on this story of the ministry of a prophet can deepen the compassion of the preacher and pastor in the ministry of grief.

Ezekiel 37:1–14 is a well-known, dramatic, and rather bizarre passage about dry bones coming to life again. In the passage, the hand of the Lord takes the prophet Ezekiel to a valley full of dry bones. He is told to prophesy to the bones, so that they will come to life again. Ezekiel does as he is told, and the bones come together. Sinews, flesh, and skin grow on the bones; and the breath of life fills the once dead bones. The passage is a parabolic message of hope to the people of Judah in the Babylonian exile, a time of deep despair. The dead bones coming back to life represent the reformulation of the community after the exile, when YHWH will breathe new spirit into the people.

This passage demonstrates the prophetic role of preaching to people who are discouraged and defeated—economically, physically, and spiritually. The author of Ezekiel demonstrates pastoral listening by quoting the people in verse 11, "Our bones are dried up, and our hope is lost; we are cut off completely." Ezekiel could speak to the discouragement of the people because he truly and deeply understood it. The unforgettable image of dry bones coming to life was intended to reawaken hope in a people with no collective energy left.

Ezekiel's remarkable words can be used in a variety of pastoral situations. This passage can be used for the feeling of defeat in personal tragedies, such as divorce, but especially in times when a disaster hits an entire community. If a tornado devastates a town, or a plant closing throws people out of work, or an arsonist burns down a church building, Ezekiel's startling images can provide a measure of comfort and encouragement. The oracles of salvation in the prophetic writings are a valuable resource for the pastoral dimensions of preaching.

The Prophets and Intercession

Although we usually think of the prophets as preaching a word of YHWH to the people, on occasion the prophets exercised a ministry of intercession. They cried out to God over the anguish of the people, or pleaded with God on their behalf. Amos interceded with God on behalf of the people, imploring God to spare Israel from the planned punishment (7:4–6). A lengthy example of pastoral intercession appears in Isaiah 63:15–64:12, where the prophet asks God to intervene in a conflict within the second temple community. With unforgettable images, the prophet pleaded with God to tear open the heavens and come down and work among the people. God responds in chapter 65, pointing out the sins of the people that created the gulf between them and God. Even though God utters words of judgment, the whole passage is a passionate dialogue between God and the people, with the prophet as mediator.

In the life of a congregation, situations arise that call for the pastor to express the needs and feelings of the congregation in intercession. The pastor can enable the congregation to lament a tragedy or an injustice. Lamentation can help a community to vent rage and frustration, a psychologically healthy and theologically sound response to pain and resentment. As Fred Craddock points out, "sermons should speak *for* as well as *to* the congregation."[6] One way of speaking for the congregation is to enable the people to express their grief, frustration, and even outrage. The prophetic tradition of lamentation is a model for that aspect of ministry.

The Prophets and Theology

When we hear the term "doctrinal preaching," we usually think of the great creeds of the church, not of the Old Testament prophets. Yet the prophets were poetic geniuses who created intriguing and even startling metaphors for God, such metaphors being the raw material of theology. Careful attention to the writings of the prophets can yield many insights for the church's theological reflection.

The most obvious doctrine on which the prophets wrote was the understanding of God. Hosea compares the relationship between God and Israel to a troubled marriage (chapters 1–3) and to a parent dealing with a rebellious child (chapter 11). Reflection on either metaphor individually, or on the juxtaposition between the two, could be a fascinating exercise in doing theology. The potential for these metaphors lies in their intimacy and emotion. God is not detached; rather, God is deeply involved in the human condition. The metaphors of the prophets can be shocking, even offensive. Hosea and Amos compare God to a wild animal (Hos. 11:10, Am. 5:19), and Hosea portrays God as maggots consuming a dead body (5:12). Because these metaphors are so unexpected, they can enliven the church's thinking about God and its preaching.

The prophets are helpful in the church's reflection on eschatology. Micah 4:1–7 (and the parallel in Isaiah 2) and Isaiah 65:17–25, for example, contain poetic promises of God's future action. These passages tell of God's intention to bring peace, justice, comity among people, and harmony within nature (including the animal kingdom) to creation. Although the prophets usually speak of God's actions within history (Isa. 65 may be an exception), these passages help the church fill out its eschatological expectations and move beyond individualistic interpretations of resurrection.

Although passages such as Isaiah 11 and Micah 5 are often thought of as "predictions" of the birth of Jesus, they originally were intended to give hope within their own contexts to their first readers. The early church looked back at these texts to help them interpret the coming of the Messiah in Jesus of Nazareth. The promises of Isaiah 11 concerning justice and righteousness, and the affirmation of Micah 5 that God works in unexpected ways, especially through what is lowly and small, helps the church to do christological reflection. God's actions in the life of Israel and Judah can be paradigms to help us understand how God was acting in the Christ-event.

The Prophets and Evangelism

This chapter opened with a report on the ministry of Dr. Billy Graham, in which he seemed to draw a contrast between evangelists and prophets. However, as the root meaning of *evangel* connotes, evangelism is the proclamation of the good news of God's grace (shown definitively in the Christ-event). And the prophets give us many examples of the proclamation of good news. Hosea compares God's forgiveness to a person welcoming back an unfaithful spouse (Hos. 1–3). Second Isaiah compares God's grace to a market where all the goods are free (Isa. 55:1) and invites the people to seek YHWH at the opportune time (v. 6). Even Amos (in the final form of the book) holds out the hope of forgiveness if the people will repent (Amos 5:4–6).

The prophets remind us that our sins are collective as well as individual and that repentance can be communal as well as personal. In the prophets we are confronted with our sins, called to repentance, and offered mercy and restoration by a God who refuses to give up on us. That message is at the heart of evangelism.

Summary

As this brief look at the writings of the prophets has shown, the prophets offer broad and deep resources upon which contemporary preachers can draw. The prophets were concerned with the total spiritual health of their communities. They were skilled diagnosticians, able to pinpoint just what kind of treatment to apply: the strong word of judgment, or the encouraging word of comfort. When the community had arrogantly wrapped itself in spiritual pride, the prophets cut through the wrapping to let the light of justice shine in. When the community's spiritual resources were drained, the prophets reconnected them to the source. When the community was confused about which god to worship and how, the prophets taught them firmly but clearly. To be a prophetic preacher is to keep a constant watch over the spiritual health of the church and to know the resources from scripture and tradition to address its needs.

CHAPTER 1

Introduction to Hosea

Hosea prophesied in the Northern Kingdom of Israel during the eighth century B.C.E., a time of great economic, social, and political changes. Under Jeroboam II, Israel enjoyed military, and, evidently, economic success (compare 2 Kings 14:23–28). According to Hosea's prophecies, however, the outward success masked spiritual problems. Hosea identified these spiritual problems as a lack of faithfulness by the people and their leaders. After Jeroboam's death, internal chaos in Israel joined with the rise of the Assyrian Empire under Tiglath-Pileser III to lead to a great upheaval in the Northern Kingdom, and its eventual dissolution in 722 B.C.E. In just a few decades, the country went from a situation of relative stability and prosperity to a period of turmoil. Hosea prophesied during much of this turbulent time. His preaching had the goal of restoring the people to faithfulness in the God who had formed them as a community.[1] The people had forgotten (or ignored) their history, no longer knowing the God who had guided them out of Egypt and through the wilderness.

The book of Hosea can be divided into three sections: chapters 1–3, chapters 4–11, and chapters 12–14. Each of these sections contains oracles of judgment followed by oracles of grace. Oracles of judgment are passages that describe God's anger, disappointment, or punishment of Israel for its sins and infidelities. Oracles of grace offer forgiveness, reconciliation, hope, and restoration. Hosea's oracles of judgment—often brusque and even crass—were intended to snap the people of Israel to attention. His oracles of grace extended healing and mercy to a people who, even though they had been complacent, were at times bewildered and frightened.

Hosea's original oracles were collected and edited over the course of about three centuries. The final form of the book was completed around the time of the Babylonian exile in the Southern Kingdom of Judah.[2] The prophet Hosea's original purpose was to call the people of Israel to fidelity to YHWH in the topsy-turvy eighth century B.C.E. Part of the intention of the subsequent editions was to help the Southern Kingdom learn from the mistakes of the Northern Kingdom of Israel.

Hosea's dynamic preaching could serve in more than one historical setting. Our concern will be primarily with the final form of the book and how the rhetorical and poetic force of the words transcends their historical context to speak afresh to a new generation.

Chapters 1 – 3

The first major section of Hosea, chapters 1–3, unfolds a bizarre and troubling–yet fascinating–metaphor. The narrator of chapter 1 explains that YHWH directs Hosea to take a "wife of whoredom." This marriage is a symbolic act, intended to reveal to the people of Israel their own infidelity to YHWH. This metaphor is fraught with difficulties for the both the scholar and the preacher. Commentators cannot reach consensus on the exact implications of the terms here rendered "wife of whoredom." The three main possibilities are that Gomer was a common prostitute, a cult prostitute, or an unfaithful wife. The further confusion is whether the "whoredom" began after the marriage, or whether Hosea knew about his bride's promiscuity, even at the altar. If the book of Hosea intends to say that the infidelity began after the marriage, then the implication is that the marriage is a metaphor for a good relationship between YHWH and Israel turned sour. If the book implies that the relationship was rocky from the start, then the homiletic message is that YHWH took a chance all along, knowing that the people of Israel were a risky gamble for a relationship.

Hosea 2:15 seems to suggest that the early relationship was a good one. Other parts of the book support the idea that the relationship was always a troubled one, with no blissful beginning to look back on. For example, in 12:2–6, Hosea's "sermon" on Jacob, Jacob's troubles begin in the womb. In either case, the passage draws a sharp contrast between YHWH's faithfulness and Israel's spiritual infidelity.

The metaphor is troubling for reasons beyond its ambiguity. The metaphor works by describing a good and faithful husband married to a sexually promiscuous woman. Even though we can draw spiritual insight from the metaphor and even though some marriages may reflect a situation somewhat similar to the one described in Hosea 1–3, the metaphor itself offends the contemporary church. The metaphor was intended to offend Israel. God through the prophet used the horrifying metaphor to shake the people out of their complacency.

For a prophet to compare a lack of spiritual vigor to sexual promiscuity is shocking in any culture. Hosea intended the shock, but the metaphor is still offensive. It offends the contemporary church because it demeans the wife's role in a marriage. We know quite well that problems in a marriage are complex, with both parties usually contributing to any dysfunction. Statistically, men are more likely than women to indulge in pornography, employ prostitutes, or commit adultery. In addition, Hosea's punishment of Gomer in chapter 2 is excessive and at least borders on abuse. If a preacher decides to approach chapters 1–3, extreme caution is recommended. (See the exegesis on pp. 24–28 in connection with the sermons on Hosea 2:14ff.)

Despite these problems, Hosea 1–3 depicts an unforgettable way of thinking about the relationship between God and God's people. If we transpose this relationship to the church, we get an intimate metaphor for reflecting on the divine-human relationship. Our sins, our shortcomings, our lack of fidelity to God cause God a pain comparable to the pain of infidelity in a marriage. God's forgiveness and love for us are not easy and casual. Our reconciliation with God is somehow similar to the awkward reunion between marriage partners after an act of betrayal.

This metaphor can be pressed too far, of course. Marriage partners are equals, peers. We are not equal with God! In some ways, though, the marriage metaphor may be more helpful to us than the parent-child metaphor with which we are more familiar because it assumes that we are adults, capable of responding maturely in a relationship.[3]

Chapters 1–3 contain a theologically significant interplay between words of judgment and words of grace and forgiveness. In chapter 1, for example, verses 1–9 describe the anger of YHWH at the people of Israel, expressed through Hosea's marriage. In verses 4–9, Hosea gives symbolic names to his children, each name revealing an aspect of God's judgment.

The first child, Jezreel, alludes to the violence of the past and predicts a violent future for Israel. The names of the second and third children announce that YHWH no longer pities the people of Israel and that they are no longer YHWH's people. These verses are a devastating judgment of the withdrawal of YHWH's favor.

Then, in verse 10, everything previously said is taken back! Instead of the kingdom of Israel coming to an end (v. 4), the people of Israel are called "Children of the living God." The two separate kingdoms are reunited. They will have land (representing security and stability), and the violence of Jezreel will be swallowed up in greatness. This see-saw pattern between judgment and grace continues with more judgment at the beginning of chapter 2.

Even though we rejoice that the fierce anger of chapters 1–3 is balanced with promises of God's ever-present favor, the transition between verse 9 and verse 10 is abrupt. Every pastor knows that the gap between verse 9 and verse 10, though small on paper, is a wide gulf, theologically. Within this gap must come a change in the people. In the space between these two verses the preacher must squeeze the genuine hearing of God's righteous judgment, heartfelt repentance, and the spiritual maturity to hear God's offer of grace as something more than mere indulgence. To blare out God's judgment and then to offer facile grace from our pulpits would bypass the growth in faith that the gap between verse 9 and verse 10 demands.

The transition between chapters 2 and 3 is again an interesting rhetorical move. At the end of chapter 2, all of the family relationships have been restored. Gomer and Hosea are reunited; the three children are welcomed back into the fold.

The relationship between Hosea and Gomer will be marked by *righteousness, justice, steadfast love,* and *mercy,* four rich theological terms.[4] The picture is one of tranquility and harmony. Then, suddenly, in chapter 3, everything falls apart. Hosea is told to go once again to love a woman who is "an adulteress." The relationship between chapters 1–2 and chapter 3 is much debated.[5]

Whether the woman in chapter 3 is Gomer or not, the editorial decision to place chapter 3 immediately after chapter 2 speaks an important word about our faith and relationship to God. As the story now reads in the book, the prophet Hosea cannot long enjoy the restored relationship of the end of chapter 2. Either with Gomer, or another woman (though most likely still with Gomer), Hosea must make himself vulnerable to hurt once again. Our own relationship with God is never static. We continue to work on our faith and receive God's grace over and over. God's grace is not offered only once, but continually, and repeatedly. Just as Hosea makes himself vulnerable again, even after the restored relationship breaks down, so God is willing to be vulnerable enough to us to enter into relationship, even after our repeated infidelities.

Chapters 4—11

This section of Hosea is not as unified by a single metaphor as chapters 1–3 are. Instead, these chapters are replete with fascinating metaphors for the relationship between YHWH and the people. In this section, oracles of judgment do not alternate with oracles of grace, as in chapters 1–3. The oracles in this section are all harsh words, hammering home YHWH's anger at the deep-seated spiritual and social problems in Israel. The word of grace comes only in chapter 11, a tender portrayal of YHWH's affection and tenacious love for Israel.

Because this section of Hosea is not as unified as the previous section and because much of the material consists of oracles of judgment, we will take a somewhat random look at some of the interesting ways that Hosea describes the people's relationship to YHWH. Most of these images, oracles, and metaphors would not make good texts for sermons by themselves, because they lack the needed word of grace.

Nevertheless, these metaphors, which come at the reader rapid-fire throughout the section, could provide important substance within a sermon.

The setting for the first three verses of chapter 4 is a courtroom. YHWH has an "indictment" against the people of Israel. This courtroom metaphor is a common theme among the prophets. (See, for example, Isa. 3:13; Am. 3:13 among many others; and see the exegesis and sermons on Mic. 6:1–8 on pp. 126–43.) Obviously, a courtroom metaphor lacks the intimacy of a marriage metaphor. YHWH is no longer a betrayed husband, but a prosecuting attorney.[6] In a marriage, the issue is working out a mutual relationship. In a courtroom, the issue is facing guilt and being confronted with specific sins.

In chapter 4, as the "charges" are read against the "defendant," Israel, we can see a clear theological progression. Verse 1c ("There is no faithfulness…") describes the underlying causes of the charge. The people's lack of faithfulness, loyalty, and knowledge of God has led to their crimes. Verse 2 gives the visible "evidence" against the people: swearing (not cursing, but taking false oaths), deceit, unfaithfulness, and violence. Verse 3 then gives the consequences of the people's actions: grief, disruption, and ecological crisis.

This passage provides keen insight into human sinfulness. Our sinful actions are rooted in deeper spiritual problems, of which we are often unaware, or only partly aware. Sermons that can identify and uncover the deeper spiritual problems will be more profoundly effective than those that stay on the surface.

If we pick up on the prophet's message about ecology, we can see the modern analogy. The root cause of our problems is greed that causes us to ignore the needs of our ecosystems. The specific acts of sin would be our many ways of polluting our environment. The consequences are worsening air quality, trashed beaches, global warming, and the subsequent illnesses caused by pollution. Preachers will be able to imagine other examples of this sequence of underlying cause-specific actions-devastation, consequences.

The section 6:1–6 is an interesting passage about the people's desire to return to YHWH. In chapter 5, Hosea's oracles have driven home the point that the people will be punished. Israel is no better than a dead body, and YHWH will consume it as maggots do a corpse (5:12). YHWH is like a lion, tearing through flesh and carrying off the game (5:14). This barrage of punishing images is intended to compel the people to repentance (5:15). In 6:1–3, the people have had enough and do, indeed, seek to return. The prophet's insight into the process is remarkable. Although the spokesperson for the people does not confess their guilt, he does acknowledge that YHWH has punished them. He understands that even though YHWH has torn and punished, YHWH will also heal and restore. YHWH's grace is dependable and leads to growth (v. 3). The reader should assume that the desire to return to YHWH is genuine, not merely a way of escaping further punishment. The people truly desire the refreshing water of grace.

Nevertheless, in verse 4, YHWH speaks. Although YHWH recognizes the sincerity of the people's need and desire for grace, YHWH knows they are not yet spiritually mature enough for genuine discipleship. YHWH's cry in verse 4 is a poignant admission that, by giving us free will, YHWH becomes vulnerable. Here YHWH feels true anguish over the people's abuse of that freedom, but will not coerce our faithfulness. YHWH's strategy of punishment has gotten the attention of the people, has softened their resistance, and has created the desire for a renewed relationship; but it has not produced the faithfulness, knowledge of God, or self-giving love that would enable the people to enter into a genuine relationship with YHWH.

Chapters 7–9 contain stinging oracles of judgment against Israel. These chapters (actually beginning at 6:7) expose Israel's sins. These oracles indicate why God is in such anguish in 6:4–6. Israel's sin is so systemic and intractable that God verges on despair over Israel's ability to rise above it. The root of Israel's sin is lack of faith. In the final form of the book these oracles lead into the offer of grace in chapter 11. Only after we understand the depth of Israel's sin do we fully appreciate God's vulnerable grace.

These chapters offer the preacher an abundance of evocative images. In a series of similes and metaphors the author drives home the destructiveness of sin. Sin makes a people useless. Israel is a cake not turned: burned on one side but raw on the other, without value as food (7:8b). Israel is like a defective bow that cannot shoot accurately (7:16). Sin leads to anxiety. Israel is like a silly dove that flits from place to place seeking security (7:11). Sin perverts worship. Altars intended for expiation of sin become altars on which to commit sin (8:11). Sin corrupts politics (8:4a, b). Preachers can use these oracles to illustrate the perversity of sin.

The first few verses of chapter 10 are a brief, but significant, passage about the seduction of success. Hosea refers to Israel as a "luxuriant vine" that yields much fruit. In the early days of Hosea's ministry, during the reign of Jeroboam II, Israel enjoyed renewed prosperity after a long period of decline. As Hosea suggests in 10:1, this material success was accompanied by the building of altars, a sign of religiosity. In verse 2, Hosea reveals the irony that the material success, and even the proliferation of altars, did not change the hearts of the people.

At the time of this writing, the United States is enjoying a prolonged period of economic expansion. Many churches are planning new buildings and expansion projects. We easily fall prey to the temptation to believe that success and expansion are sure signs of God's favor.

Hosea bursts our bubble by declaring that new altars (and new church buildings) do not necessarily mean that hearts have been changed. Economic expansion usually means that jobs are plentiful, and a good economy often eases the stresses that exacerbate some social ills. New and renovated church buildings enable the church to perform its mission efficiently. Nevertheless, economic growth and building projects do not guarantee that all is well with the people of God.

Chapters 12—14

The wonderful passage in chapter 11 would have made a fine ending for the book of Hosea. In chapter 11, God decides to end the punishment of exile, not to destroy Israel, and to act on Israel's behalf. The people return to their land to enjoy security and stability, much as they do at the end of chapter 2. As happened in chapter 3, however, the editor of Hosea begins a new cycle of oracles of judgment. The reader is reminded of the unfinished business of true discipleship. After presenting the word of grace, the editor plunges the reader back into the midst of the reality of judgment. Two passages from this section deserve special attention: 12:2–6 and 14:1–7.

Passage 12:2–6 is a poetic "sermon" on Jacob. For the historical-critical scholar, this passage indicates that some form of the Jacob story preceded the writing of Hosea. For the contemporary preacher, this passage gives an example of how the prophet interpreted tradition for a new situation, the pastor's weekly task. Hosea does not follow the order of the story we have today in Genesis. Either he had a different version of the story, or he employed a kind of "homiletic license" to change the story to fit his purposes.

Within the sermon, Hosea details Jacob's movement from sin to restoration. The passage starts out with the courtroom motif again, as chapter 4 did. According to the sermon, Jacob's transgressions began in the womb when he tried to supplant Esau. As an adult, he "strove" with God, continuing the lifelong conflict within himself and between him and God.

Although Hosea writes cryptically, verse 4 seems to represent a turning point in Jacob's development. The text says that Jacob met "him" at Bethel, and from verse 5, one would infer that the "him" is God. The poem seems to be saying that after a lifetime of conflict, Jacob had a transforming experience with God. The poem encourages a similar experience for the people, who have acted unfaithfully for their whole existence.

The preacher addresses the congregation directly in verse 6 and presents the elements of a proper response to an experience with God. These elements are to "hold fast to love and justice," and to "wait continually for your God." The content of this verse is a good summary of prophetic faith and bears much similarity to Micah 6:8.

Chapter 13 presents an angry image of God. Throughout the book of Hosea God has shown a mixture of emotions. God has been hurt, frustrated, and angry. Here in chapter 13, anger is the dominant emotion. The author portrays God as one dangerous wild beast after another (13:7–8). The Assyrian army will be God's instrument of judgment. The soldiers will spare neither infants nor pregnant women.

Verse 14 presents complications for translation and interpretation. God addresses "Death" and "Sheol" directly. Using personification the author represents them as forces with destructive power. The complication is the translation of the word rendered "compassion" in the last line of verse 14. The word can mean vengeance. If the word is translated as "compassion," God is threatening to unleash the forces of chaos with no compassion to restrain their destruction. If the word is translated as "vengeance," God has decided to practice restraint. The context of the passage suggests that "compassion" is the correct translation. God will release the full fury of Death and Sheol.

Preachers should be careful in using these images. God is angry at sin, but God's wrath is tempered by grace. Many people have been turned off from the church by preachers who made inappropriate threats. God's wrath is especially aimed at the powerful, not mischievous teenagers or struggling young adults. In the final form of Hosea, God's wrath in chapter 13 is mitigated by the promise of redeeming love in chapter 14.

The final chapter of Hosea is, as would be expected, a message of salvation. The book has piled up image after image, metaphor after metaphor, in an attempt to diagnose the sins of Israel and Judah and to break down the people's denial. Now, 14:1-7 announces again the word of salvation. The language of this passage is the language of worship. In fact, I venture that it is not too much of an exaggeration to identify the elements of a worship service in this passage. Verse 1 serves as the call to worship; 2a is the call to confession; 2b-3b is the prayer of confession; 3c is the declaration of pardon; verses 4-7 form the sermon. The book of Hosea, as it now stands, has been seeking to move the reader to a genuine experience with God that will result in a life of discipleship and the establishment of community. How appropriate, then, that the book closes with the elements of worship. Genuine worship is rooted in an experience with God that leads to community, the pursuit of justice, and a discipleship that reaches out to others.

The content of the brief sermon (verses 4–7) promises God's action on behalf of, within, and among the people. God's anguished cry in 6:4 ("What shall I do with you?") is here answered. If the people are too spiritually immature to form a relationship with God, God will act to "heal their disloyalty." Just as the book has piled images and metaphors for sin and disobedience on top of one another, so the final sermon piles metaphors for growth and development one upon another. God will be like dew that causes plants to grow. The plants shall grow deep roots, send out sturdy branches, blossom, and fill the air with a sweet fragrance.

Theological Reflection on Preaching Hosea

Hosea's oracles of judgment sting as sharply as those of any of the prophets. The people of Israel are like a sexually promiscuous person (chapters 1–3), like an overheated oven (7:4–7), like a cake cooked on one side but raw on the other (7:8), even like a dead body waiting to rot (5:12). Hosea doesn't hold back in denouncing the people's infidelity.

Hosea escapes the snare of self-righteousness, however, because he is willing to share the people's pain. Hosea himself enters into a marriage, knowing that his wife will betray him. Hosea reveals a God who is indeed angry, but also in deep anguish over the people's recalcitrance (6:4; 11:8). That sense of anguish from both Hosea and God gives the prophecies of this book a poignant authority. We are not just trying to avoid God's wrath and punishment; we are called to enter into a relationship with God, who is both spouse and parent.

That relationship requires a response on our part. For Hosea, that response consists of fidelity, steadfast love, justice, and the knowledge of God. Although these four terms do not exhaust Hosea's expected response from the people of Israel, they are a good summary of the essence of Hosea's ethical message. The most consistent accusation Hosea makes against the people is that they are not completely faithful to YHWH. Hosea says, "Ephraim is joined to idols" (4:17, see also 4:12–13), meaning that they worship YHWH *and* the gods of the surrounding peoples. Preachers can reflect on ways that the contemporary church, without completely abandoning the faith, worships other gods along with worship of the risen Christ (see discussion on p. 42 in chapter 11). One of the most well-known verses from Hosea is 6:6, "For I desire steadfast love and not sacrifice, / the knowledge of God rather than burnt offerings" (see Matt. 9:13 and 12:7). By using the word for "steadfast love," Hosea here exhorts Israel to consistent, dependable, active love for God and other people.[7] "Knowledge of God" refers to a deep, abiding, intimate relationship with God.[8] Justice is not as prominent a theme in Hosea as it is in Amos and Micah. Nevertheless, 12:6 lists justice as an integral part of the people's witness. Justice is essential fairness—in the courts, in business, and in access to goods.

Hosea issues YHWH's judgment on the people and outlines an ethical response, but the final word in Hosea—in each of the three sections, and at the end of the book—is grace. Two important terms for Hosea are "mercy" (2:19) and "compassion" (11:8). The first of these terms (also sometimes translated as "compassion") refers to God's forgiveness, healing, and favor (see Pss. 77:9 and 103:4). One use of the term in Proverbs 12:10 (a lack of compassion for animals) suggests that it refers to how a being treats those in a dependent relationship. YHWH shows such mercy to Israel. The second term, "compassion," can also refer to comfort (Isa. 57:18). Both terms convey God's active love working to forgive Israel and restore the relationship. YHWH will not only hang in there with the people and continue to love them in spite of their infidelity, YHWH will also work within and among the people to heal them. YHWH has shown steadfast love in the exodus, in the wilderness, in the formation of the people; and YHWH will continue to love the people, even if they are unfaithful, until that love transforms them.

CHAPTER 2

Hosea 2:14–23

Exegesis

Preaching from the second chapter of Hosea might be compared to leaning over a railing to get a view of a spectacular landscape. The beauty of the landscape is worth the risk, but if you do not watch your step…YHWH's romantic treatment of Israel in the second half of the chapter is wonderful to behold, but the severe treatment YHWH subjects Israel to in the first half requires us to step carefully and not to lean too far over the railing.

In English, the division between the two halves of the chapter comes at the end of verse 13. (In Hebrew the division comes between verses 15 and 16. All subsequent references will be to the English versification.) The whole chapter employs a family metaphor, with YHWH as the husband/father and Israel as both the wayward wife *and* her children. This chapter follows the command in chapter 1 for Hosea to marry Gomer, a "wife of whoredom." As discussed above in the introduction to Hosea, Hosea's marriage to Gomer is an enacted judgment on Israel. Gomer bears three children, who are given symbolic names: *Jezreel* (the site of a bloody battle), *Lo-ruhamah* (no pity), and *Lo-ammi* (not my people). By the end of chapter 1, God promises forgiveness and reconciliation. Now in chapter 2, words of judgment begin again, continuing the metaphor of a troubled marriage. The first half of chapter 2 describes YHWH's punishment of Israel for her apostasy and infidelity. In the second part of the chapter, YHWH forgives the "wife" Israel and reconciles with her.

The pitfalls for the preacher contained in the first half of the chapter are enormous. If we are to explore the beauty of the reconciliation between YHWH and Israel in the second half of the chapter, we must decide how to avoid the pitfalls in the first half. Although the husband/wife relationship in the chapter is only metaphorical, the description of YHWH's punishment of the "wife" Israel comes dangerously close to spousal abuse.[1]

YHWH threatens to strip Israel naked (v. 3), to entrap her (v. 6), deprive her (vv. 3, 9), and shame her (v. 10). The treatment of the three children, who also serve as metaphors for Israel, is at least as problematic as the treatment of the wife, if not more so. YHWH, the "father," rejects them because of their mother's infidelity (v. 4). Even if we acknowledge the cultural differences between the patriarchal ancient Israelite society and today, to portray God in this punishing way is dangerous. Women and children who have endured abuse would likely be repulsed by such an image of God. The preacher must hold on tightly to the railing at this point.

An important question of interpretation is how the authors/editors of Hosea understood the punishment of Israel in verses 1–13. Certainly the punishment was not an end in itself, because it gave way to the rekindled romance. Likewise, we should reject any interpretation that suggests that YHWH is capricious, unpredictable, or given to mood swings: angry one minute, gentle the next. In one sense, the punishment in the wilderness prepares Israel for the renewed relationship. Israel must be shown that her infidelity is wrong.

Even so, the text does not say that Israel repents and that the repentance leads to the romantic treatment of the second half of the chapter. Apparently, YHWH eschews punishment as ineffective, opting for the seductive strategy beginning in verse 14. A true relationship cannot be built on punishment. This passage makes the daring claim that God chooses to "court" Israel, hoping to "win" her away from the Baals. We must also remember that the relationship is a metaphor. With that in mind, we can affirm that God's punishment is not vindictive, but purging and preparatory.

In a sermon, a preacher could draw an analogy between the punishment in verses 1–13 and the suffering we cause ourselves, or that simply happens to us, a suffering that can lead us to seek God. Just as tension and conflict in a marriage are inevitable, so are times in our lives when we feel estranged from God. We all have wilderness experiences in which, even if we aren't being punished, we feel abandoned, or at least distant, from God. Hosea says that God comes to that wilderness to win us back.

The transition between verses 13 and 14 is quite abrupt. Following the punishment of verses 1–13, YHWH suddenly decides to "allure" Israel into a revitalized relationship (v. 14). The Hebrew word for "allure" carries connotations of enticement and seduction. In Proverbs 1:10, the word refers to sinners who tempt a naive young person down the wrong path. In Judges 16:5, it describes Delilah's wiles in coaxing Samson to reveal the secret of his strength. The term carries a certain naughtiness. Hosea 2:14 envisions a scene of sly smiles, meaningful glances, dimmed lights, and playful giggles. The renewed relationship between YHWH and Israel will be tender and intimate. YHWH's new strategy of seduction is the dominant metaphor of the second half of the chapter.

The metaphor of seduction is important for two reasons. It speaks first of God's emotional investment in the relationship with Israel and, by extension, with the church. God is not detached and far off. God willingly enters a relationship of love, in which God is vulnerable to hurt. Secondly, the metaphor of seduction preserves Israel's power. One is always free to reject seduction, however tempting it might be. Although Israel's punishment in 2:1–13 is severe, in the end, YHWH does not overpower Israel. "She" is invited to join willingly in the renewed relationship.

As part of the restored relationship, YHWH gives back to Israel all that YHWH took away during the time of punishment. In 2:9 Israel is deprived of wine and grain; in 2:15, 22 YHWH gives back the grain and wine. In 2:7 Israel is frustrated in pursuing her lovers; in 2:16–17 YHWH removes the names of the Baals from her mouth. In 2:12 nature is a hostile, punishing force; in 2:18 YHWH establishes a covenant between Israel and the wild animals. In 2:2–4 the family is broken, with even the children bearing the consequences; in 2:19–23 the family is restored to wholeness.

Verses 19-20 give the romantic relationship metaphor an important theological interpretation. The reconciliation is described with a succession of important theological terms. The relationship will last "forever," indicating stability, and will be marked by "righteousness," "justice," "steadfast love," "mercy," and "faithfulness." Israel will know YHWH. These terms describe the relationship between YHWH and Israel, but also conditions within Israel. Because YHWH will take the initiative, Israelite society will be characterized by fairness, equality, self-giving, and dependable love, compassion, and concern for the poor and for outcasts. If Israel is to know YHWH, Israel will have a close relationship with YHWH. Each will understand the other's true nature. Romance is an important metaphor for this passage, but the relationship leads to ethical, social, and spiritual harmony.

The rekindled romance between YHWH and Israel extends in an eschatological direction affecting all of creation. The earth, which had suffered during the time of punishment, will produce the nourishing staples of life (v. 23). YHWH will bring an end to war and destruction (v. 18b), and harmony will prevail within nature (v. 18a). The passage that begins with a beckoning wink ends in peace for all of heaven and earth.

This tricky but intriguing passage can be preached on many levels. The stormy but reconciled relationship between YHWH and Israel can serve as an analogy on an individual level, on the level of the church, or for God's relationship to the creation (and all creatures) itself. On the individual level, this passage could speak to people who feel abandoned, punished, or rejected by God.

While being careful not to portray God as abusive, the preacher can connect the feeling of abandonment by, or distance from, God with the punishment of Israel in verses 1-13. Care must be taken not to suggest that all suffering is punishment for sin. Such a sermon could point the hearers toward a new and closer relationship with God. A clear analogy can be drawn between the restored relationship between Israel and YHWH and the restorative grace God offers the church. In spite of the church's unfaithfulness, God will not give up on it. Rather, God works to restore the relationship and use the church to foster justice, righteousness, and the knowledge of God.

Because the passage contains such a strong eschatological dimension, a preacher can use it to talk of God's healing of all creation and of reconciliation with (and among) all creatures. God will renew nature despite humankind's pollution. God will establish peace despite our wars. If God's children, understood as all of humanity, have abandoned God and been unfaithful, God will renew the relationship.

Sermon

"A Second Honeymoon"

United Methodist pastors and their churches usually meet for the first time at a "seating" set up by the district superintendent. The pastor-parish (or staff-parish) relations committee and other leaders of the church meet with the pastor (and spouse and children, as the case may be). Usually, a seating is a warm, gracious affair, with best feet being put forward, a smile on every face, animated conversation, and the planting of the seeds of a new relationship.

Let's use our imaginations to conjure up a possible scenario for a United Methodist seating. You are free to use whatever helps you get your imagination going—closing your eyes or whatever. Now, as we start our imaginative journey, we need a word of warning.

Our text is from Hosea. Hosea is an unusual prophet; he can make people blush, even when he is preaching. At one point in his book, he refers to the people of Israel as a dead body and God as a maggot, eating the dead body. He never heard the advice about not mentioning sex and politics in church. If we want to get a picture of what Hosea would be like today, what we should do is take a little bit of DNA from Billy Graham and mix in a little DNA from Eddie Murphy. Then we could clone Hosea. So, with that warning, let's begin our imaginary seating at a United Methodist church.

The pastor-parish relations committee of our fictional United Methodist church has gotten everything prepared for the seating. The church has been cleaned top to bottom; the best linens have been put out; finger food has been prepared;

fresh coffee has been brewed. The men on the committee have on their best suits. Shirts are ironed, and ties straightened—in some cases with a wife's help. The women are in their best dresses, and everyone has been to the hairstylist. An air of anticipation fills the room as everyone waits for the new pastor to arrive.

Right on time, she comes in with a big smile on her face. Everyone on the committee is immediately impressed by her warmth and confidence. In addition to her good first impression, she has a dynamite resume: master's degree with honors from Duke and doctoral degree from SMU. Her previous church had a 40 percent increase in worship attendance over the last five years. She has won an award for her preaching. Before she went into the ministry, she was a kindergarten teacher and loves kids. All-in-all, the committee is delighted with the cabinet's choice. By the way, her husband also attends the meeting. He is stylishly dressed, and everyone notices—especially the women on the committee—that he is, well, tall and ruggedly handsome.

As the evening moves along, the conversation turns toward the new pastor's personal history. Where had she grown up? What were her hobbies? How long had she and her husband been married? Speaking of her husband, he has been rather quiet all evening.

One of the committee members tries to get him to open up, asking what she thinks will be an innocent question: "What do you do for a living?" With the husband's answer, everything changes. "Oh," the husband responds matter-of-factly, "I star in adult movies."

A sudden chill goes through the room. The committee members squirm uncomfortably in their seats. Nobody knows quite what to say. That is not the answer they expected. Finally, one of the committee members says to the new pastor, "We've never had a minister whose spouse made adult movies before. We're not sure what to think about that."

The young pastor is quiet for a moment, and then says,

> I know you all are shocked by what my husband does for a living. It bothers me sometimes, too. But I believe God wants me to stay with my husband. The tawdry

movies my husband makes are a judgment against the church. The church's love for God is as artificial and insincere as the cheap love portrayed in his movies. My husband's movies show images of a kind of 'love' that makes no commitment, develops no real relationship. It is a shallow love that cares only for momentary pleasure. Too many people in the church have a shallow love for God. They care only for what God can give them, without making any real commitment, without giving anything back. When the people in the church see my husband, I want them to ask if their love for God is any better than the love shown in his movies.

After that explanation, the committee reluctantly decides to accept the appointment of this pastor made by the cabinet and bishop. With nagging doubts in the back of their minds, they welcome their new pastor. From the very beginning, she does an outstanding job. She visits so much that the people wonder how she has time to write her sermons. Even so, her sermons are moving and inspiring. The children race to the altar each Sunday for her children's sermons. First-time visitors comment on how friendly she is and how much they like her.

Nevertheless, no one can forget her husband and what he does for a living. He's an embarrassment to the church and community. The people in the church know that everyone in town is talking behind their backs. No one in the church knows what to say to him at potluck fellowships. Everyone is uncomfortable, but they keep reminding themselves of what the pastor said that first night in her seating, that her marriage is a judgment against the church. Her husband is a constant reminder that God wants genuine love, not insincere mush, true commitment, not casual affection. So, the members take that message to heart, put up with the talking behind their backs, and sometimes really do ask themselves how strong their love for God is.

A time comes when the people begin to notice that the pastor is off her game. She looks tired and doesn't seem as upbeat as she did at first. Her sermons aren't as compelling as they used to be. One Sunday, she announces that she and her husband will take an extended vacation together. She has arranged for guest preachers for a month and for someone to do emergency pastoral visitation.

When the pastor and her husband return from vacation, she is her old self again: energetic, lively, inspiring in the pulpit. At first she is reticent about discussing the vacation. Finally, though, after enough people ask her how she got her old self back, she preaches a sermon about it. The vacation had not started off very peacefully. She was tired of being married to an adult film star, and she told her husband that. She wanted him to quit, but he refused. They spent most of the vacation arguing. Things got so heated that she didn't know if the marriage would survive.

By the last week, though, he started to listen. When she realized that she had his attention, she said the words that melted his resistance and touched his heart. She looked right at him and asked, "Don't you know how much I love you, much more than the women in your movies ever could? Don't you know that what we have is real, that I would do anything for you, that you mean the world to me?"

When her husband heard those words, he knew he had made his last movie. He decided then and there to find another job and to show his wife the devoted love she deserved. The marriage was healed. He was baptized and joined the church. As far as the young pastor was concerned, all was right with heaven and earth.

This parable about a United Methodist pastor may sound bizarre, but it is the story of Hosea's life. Hosea is the strange, but obedient prophet given the almost incomprehensible command from God to marry a fallen woman. His marriage is to serve as a judgment to Israel about their own unfaithfulness. The people of Israel tried to worship God *and* other gods. Chapter 1 describes Hosea's marriage to Gomer, a marriage that embodies Israel's spiritual unfaithfulness. The first part of chapter 2 describes God's anger at Israel. At first, God gets rough with Israel, to try to get her attention. But God can't stay angry for long.

In the passage we read for this morning, God takes his unfaithful wife Israel on a second honeymoon. The language of verse 14 is the language of romance. God says, "I will…allure her…and speak tenderly to her." Their love will be as fresh and spontaneous as the love of newlyweds. God will show Israel that his love is better than the love of idols can ever be. The newly found romance will be a time of celebration. Not only will the couple celebrate, but all of creation will join them. The heavens and the earth will rejoice.

Doesn't Hosea sound like Luke here? Luke tells about a shepherd who goes in search of one lost sheep. When he finds it, he calls his friends and neighbors to rejoice with him. Luke also tells of a woman who searches for a lost coin. When she finds it, she gets her friends to rejoice with her. Luke says that when one sinner repents, heaven throws a party, and all the angels join in.

Maybe our relationship with God isn't what we want it to be. Maybe what was once a strong, vibrant love affair between God and us has grown stale, routine, and dull. Maybe we want a love for God that is fresh, new, and spontaneous. Maybe we want a love for God that will help us love others and reach out to those in need. If so, God beckons us to fall in love again.

God's love will allure us from our sins and from our flirtations with the evil of the world. Today is a good time to ask if anger at God has kept us from enjoying our love for God. Have we been too busy for God? Have we let the warm glow of our relationship with God flicker out? If our love for God has been too shallow, too insincere, too uncommitted, if we need a stronger or deeper relationship with God, then God has plane tickets and hotel reservations for our second honeymoon.

SERMON

"A Marriage Made in Heaven and Broken on Earth"

A. Carter Shelley

Introduction

The book of the prophet Hosea contains two powerful metaphors. The second introduces God as a loving parent in chapter 11: "When Israel was a child, I loved him." The first metaphor is that of a marriage between God and God's people. As Hosea relates it, this is not a blissful marriage. These "newlyweds" are not Jessica Simpson and Nick Lachey. The marital problems are better suited to the steamy, seamy world of *Desperate Housewives* than they are to our own "happily ever after" assumptions. And we must remember that the words Hosea utters are not human in origin but come from God.

(Read Hosea 2:14–23.)

The marriage metaphor of the wanton, wayward, whoring wife and the loving, faithful, and much-injured husband describes the story of God's marital contract with Israel. This relationship began with the rescue of the Hebrew slaves from Egypt, then was codified by the exchange of vows at the Sinai Covenant, and later continued into the Israelites' life as a loosely organized group of tribes, before they became a neophyte kingdom under Saul, David, and Solomon. Now, in the eighth century B.C.E. Israel has reached a midlife crisis.

In settled Israel, the love and loyalty of Yahweh were taken for granted. Frequently, they were exchanged for the novelty and excitement of the Canaanite god, Baal, and an open marriage. As a husband, Baal made only one demand: participation in his fertility rites. Regardless of whether participation in these rites was real or symbolic, the result was the same: desertion of a faithful, loving spouse to couple with a new lover. Offered a choice between "the magical and cultic world of Canaan and the moral statutes of [God's] covenant,"[2] many Israelites preferred the glitter to the same old, same old. Their actions were not unlike the modern-day practice of trading in a well-worn spouse of twenty or so years for a newer, more exciting trophy model.

Of course, a huge divide separates divine passion and faithfulness from human fickleness and faithlessness. We aren't God. We're human. We're human, just as those Israelites were who wanted to hedge their bets on a good wheat crop by paying obeisance to Baal's fertility rites, seeking a little extra insurance just in case the God of Abraham, Isaac, and Jacob didn't come through. Not wanting to rely too heavily on God's promise of protection and prosperity, they participated in the fertility rites to guarantee their crops. They made alliances with foreign countries to protect them from invading empires in situations not dissimilar to our own international alliances and calculated financial support to buy loyalty from second and third world countries.

Whether we're discussing eighth-century Israelites or twenty-first–century Americans, we are all afraid to trust God to fulfill God's marital promises. Why? Because we view God's commitment through the tarnished, cynical eyes of humans better acquainted with betrayal and broken promises than with unconditional love and acceptance. Thus, we abandon God before God has a chance to abandon us.

Yet Hosea assures us that God is the devout husband. God will not desert us no matter how crummy we are. God's devotion is so great! God, our husband, will take us back despite all we've done. Check off the list in your life: humiliating God, denying God's existence, blaspheming God's name, and piercing God's heart with our self-centered seeking after self-gratification and false security. God, the faithful husband, with Israel (and us), the faithless wife—it's a metaphor unique to Hosea and potent in its message.

As you know, the prophets didn't prophesy just to hear the sound of their own voices. They served as interpreters of God's will. In Hosea 2:2–13, the verses that precede today's reading, the prophet condemns Israel's harlotry and outlines the consequences of her actions. God will take back the grain, wine, and oil, that is the earthly food and other necessities the Israelites hoped to insure by their worship of Baal. God will also uncover Israel's shame—exposing her to other nations as small, vulnerable, and helpless without God. In this way, God will punish Israel both for her harlotry and for disregarding her marital vows.

These words of retribution have disturbed Old Testament feminist scholars. Prominent Old Testament scholar Gale A. Yee warns that these words recounting divine punishment provide the opportunity for earthly husbands to justify abuse of their earthly wives.[3] If Hosea says a faithless wife deserves punishment, then it's O.K. to beat my wife, order her about, and expect her to be humble, repentant, subservient, and under my control.

Reinforcement for this disturbing reading of the text can be found in the fact that Hosea chose to speak of God as a husband instead of portraying God as a wife. However, Hosea chose this analogy not as a way to declare man more Godlike than woman or to claim man's superiority over women. Hosea's purpose is to speak most clearly to those in Israel with the power and the influence to change their adulterous religious and political behavior: the men. A woman living in Israel had no power or influence except through the men she was related to: first her father and brothers, later her husband and sons. Status for women came from bearing sons and little else.

Thus, a woman was in no position to question or challenge the sexual conduct of her husband. It didn't matter if Israelite men had more than one wife. It didn't matter if a man had an extramarital affair, so long as it wasn't with some other man's wife. Sex outside marriage bore none of the shame or blame for men that it held for women, who could actually be executed for such an act. The twenty-first–century American ideal of marriage as a mutually loving, mutually giving, and mutually supportive relationship had no counterpart in eighth-century Israel. They had no such concept of an equal partnership. Consequently, to have depicted God as the faithful, tender, loving wife to an adulterous husband would be too alien a concept for the men of Israel to understand.

Nor could the Israelites conceive of themselves as equal partners with God. Yahweh, the God of the Sinai Covenant and the God of the Northern Kingdom, never was their equal. God was their superior. Yet God chooses to establish a partnership between equals instead of a dictatorship. What is unique is not the human idolatry in following Baal, but the divine humility of God.

Whether describing God in the eighth-century words of Hosea or in the language of today, the fact is God the Creator, the All-Powerful, All-Knowing, and All-Controlling Holy Other chooses humility and vulnerability. God chooses to give human beings the freedom to dally with Baal or to be seduced by twenty-first–century equivalents: money, status, sex, power, fame, self. The God Hosea depicts does not force the Israelites to want God or to love God. Their response is voluntary.

They may respond with faithfulness and devotion, or they can respond with disregard and indifference.

Israel, the wife in Hosea 2, faces severe consequences due to her own actions. The earthly consequences include famine, loss of reputation, and loss of self-respect. We also have to face the consequences of our faithlessness when we settle for the ways of this world over the will of God.

Yet God seeks us out. God wants us back. God arrives with the heart-shaped box of valentine candy and flowers. God woos us, because God loves us and won't leave us:

> Therefore, I will now allure her,
>   and bring her into the wilderness,
>   and speak tenderly to her.
> From there I will give her her vineyards,
>   and make the Valley of Achor a door of hope.
> There she shall respond as in the days of her youth,
>   as at the time when she came out of the land of Egypt.
> (2:14–15)

Hosea's account of the faithful husband and the faithless wife would have led to one and only one conclusion in his own day: the stoning of the woman. That was the man's right. It is also, by implication, God's right. Instead, God identifies the consequences that such behavior causes, and chooses forgiveness rather than vengeance. God wants the marriage to work. In fact, God wants to reaffirm the marriage vows, restore the broken relationship, and deepen the commitment. The covenant God offers is glorious! Not only does God promise intimacy, understanding, tenderness, and love, but God also promises that the whole world in which people live will be altered:

> "I will make for you a covenant on that day with the wild animals, the birds of the air, and the creeping things of the ground; and I will abolish the bow, the sword, and war from the land; and I will make you lie down in safety. And I will take you for my wife forever; I will take you for my wife in righteousness and in justice, in steadfast love, and in mercy. I will take you for my wife

in faithfulness; and you shall know the LORD."
(2:18–20)

With those promises before the children of Israel and us, Hosea shifts from portraying God as husband to revealing God as fully God:

> On that day I will answer, says the LORD,
> I will answer the heavens
> and they shall answer the earth;
> and the earth shall answer the grain, the wine, and
> the oil,
> and they shall answer Jezreel;
> and I will sow him for myself in the land.
> And I will have pity on Lo-ruhamah, [*Not pitied*]
> and I will say to Lo-ammi, [*Not my people*] "You are
> my people";
> and he shall say, "You are my God.
> (2:21–23)

We live after the fall of Israel to Assyria in 722 B.C.E. We live after God's greatest act of love: God's son Jesus, who became human and dwelt among us to model the life God wills, and then died and was resurrected to share that life. We live after the brutality of Stalin's purges and Hitler's Holocaust. We live in the time of Rwanda, Serbia, and Afghanistan. While we may not have willed anything half so dreadful or bad as these crimes of the twentieth and twenty-first centuries, we, too, need reclaiming. We need to be yanked out of the pettiness of gossip, out of the treadmill tasks and demands of jobs, and out of daily life that wears us out too much to be civil or loving toward our families and friends. We need to be pulled away from the shallowness of present-day television, away from the present-day preoccupation with money and material goods, and away from the ongoing denial of our national greediness in using up so much of the world's resources. We need to be prodded out of the doldrums of depression and out of a sense of fatalism that keeps us from interacting with others and living life in all its fullness and zest. In short, we need to be pulled back into the arms of God. We need to be silenced, stroked, held, and loved so that we, too, may believe life has both a purpose and a meaning–a purpose that can be found in the passion and compassion God shares with us and expects of us.

Thanks be to a God who loves us like a Husband, saves us like the Son, and redeems us as only a God can. Amen.

CHAPTER 3

Hosea 11:1-11

Exegesis

Reading Hosea 11 is somewhat like finding a tape recording of a valuable and historic message, but discovering that the tape is badly damaged. The message on the tape is so powerful that we are compelled to listen, even if the hissing, popping, and garbled words make listening difficult. Hosea 11 is a beautiful and moving testimony of God's anguish over the sin of Israel. God struggles between judgment and mercy, in heartfelt pain over the people's rejection and idolatry. That poignant struggle comes through in this passage, even though the Hebrew text is very difficult to translate, and despite the fact that no consensus exists on the exact metaphors and allusions Hosea makes in this poem. Even though the preacher must be careful in handling this perplexing oracle, Hosea 11 furnishes a rich resource for preaching. (See below for a description of these difficulties.)

Hosea 11 was intended to give hope to the people of the Northern Kingdom of Israel near the end of the eighth century B.C.E. Under Tiglath-Pileser III, Assyria had grown into a formidable military power. He began a ruthless expansion of his territory and soon threatened Israel. At the time the oracle in Hosea 11 was proclaimed Israel was already under siege, but the capital city of Samaria had not yet fallen (an event that did happen in 722/721, when Shalmaneser V and then Sargon led Assyria). In earlier oracles, Hosea had warned Israel that God's judgment was coming. Then, when judgment came upon them,

Hosea assured the people of Israel that despite God's wrath, God had not abandoned them.

The passage is built around the metaphor of a parent's relation with a son. Other metaphors and similes fill in the picture, but the dominant metaphor is parent-child. The passage contrasts the tender, loving actions of the parent with the rebellious and ungrateful response of the son. Hosea intermingles historical allusions, such as the exodus event (v. 1), Sodom and Gomorrah (v. 8), and the current Assyrian crisis (v. 11), with metaphorical depictions of a parent's love (vv. 3–4). Despite the consistent and obvious acts of love, the "son," Israel, has rejected the love the parent offered, and has turned to Baal worship. God's initial reaction to this disobedience is punishment (vv. 5–7). The turning point of the passage is verse 8, where God struggles with the possibility of completely abandoning Israel and allowing the Assyrians to destroy it permanently. God's deep love for Israel and God's nature as one who does not abandon a son triumph in the struggle as God decides that the punishment will be temporary. After a time in exile, the Israelites will return home. God will roar like a lion, and the people will return like trembling birds in the spring.

Preaching from Hosea 11

Despite its powerful overall message, Hosea 11 presents a number of challenges in moving from the text to a contemporary Christian congregation. As noted above, parts of the passage, especially verses 3–4, are difficult to translate and interpret. In addition, several aspects of Hosea's thought and situation do not translate easily into North American churches in the twenty-first century. Three of these aspects are the problem of idolatry, the Old Testament understanding of the relationship between parents and children, and the political and military threat that Assyria posed to Israel. These problems must be handled carefully in preaching from this pericope.

Verses 1–2 establish the dominant metaphor of the poem as a parent-child relationship. YHWH is the loving parent; Israel is the recalcitrant child. The question with which translators and interpreters have wrestled is whether that metaphor extends into verses 3 and 4, or whether Hosea mixes metaphors. The Hebrew in these verses is confusing.[1] The first part of verse 3 contains a rare Hebrew word in a rare verbal form (tirgalti), the translation of which is uncertain. It is often rendered as "teach to walk." The next three words literally say, "he took them upon his forearms." *The New Revised Standard Version* Bible (NRSV) interprets verse 3 as a parent teaching a child to walk, holding his arms to keep him from falling. The Anchor Bible considers this verse to be a reference to removing the Egyptian shackles of slavery from the arms of the Israelites during the exodus.[2]

The confusion continues in verse 4. In the first part of the verse, the text literally says, "with cords of a human I drew them with ropes of love." The second half of the verse contains a Hebrew word that can mean either "yoke," "jaw," or "cheek," and a verb that means "to cause to eat." This talk of cords, ropes, and yokes has led some commentators to assume that a new metaphor has been introduced here: a farmer treating beasts of burden with kindness. Under this assumption, the farmer eases the yoke on the animal, so that it can feed. (See the RSV.) The NRSV considers this verse to be a reference to holding an infant tenderly to one's cheek and feeding him.[3]

The preacher confronts a bewildering choice of possibilities for interpretation of these two verses. The text might refer consistently to a parent-child relationship, or it might contain two metaphors (parent and farmer), or it might be a parent-child metaphor with a brief allusion to the exodus. The preacher must weigh the evidence to the best of her or his ability and decide what the text says. I am most persuaded by the argument that the parent-child metaphor continues through verse 4.

A preacher who decides that Hosea mixes his metaphors should be careful not to confuse the congregation with too many images in a sermon. To talk of a parent's love for a child and a farmer's good treatment of an animal might be too much for one sermon. In any case, the emphasis in verses 1–4 is to give examples of YHWH's love for Israel.

The parent-child metaphor in this passage, for all of its power and tenderness, may be cause for resistance in contemporary congregations. The background of the passage is the ancient law that permitted a parent to kill a stubborn child (Deut. 21:18–21).[4] In Hosea 11, YHWH is making the case that Israel is the stubborn son who deserves to die. This practice would be offensive to modern congregations. Besides that, twenty-first–century Christians are aware of social-science research indicating that "problem" children are a symptom of dysfunction in the whole family system.

The preacher should reflect carefully on how to present the issue of the church's and the individual Christian's rebellion against God. It is my experience that, for most of us, our response to God is a mixture of obedience and rebellion. Much of our sin comes from weakness as well as outright defiance of God. In a sermon, the preacher should offer a nuanced understanding of our estrangement and alienation from God.

As the Old Testament prophets frequently do, Hosea accuses the Israelites of idolatry, of turning from YHWH to worship "the Baals."[5] When Baal is used as a proper noun,[6] it refers to a god or gods of the Canaanites, Israel's neighbors. The problem for the people of Israel was not that they intentionally rejected YHWH in favor of Baal, but that they were lax in the exclusive worship of YHWH. They practiced a casual syncretism that mixed elements of Baal-worship with YHWH-worship. Because Baal worship concentrated on fertility, the Israelites were constantly tempted to offer some homage to Baal in the hopes of securing a good crop and numerous children.

Today, as in Hosea's day, how we worship and whom we worship helps determine the quality of our faith. Although only a few people in the church consciously reject the Christian faith, the church does face the problem of distorted views of the Triune God and that of the blending of Christian doctrine with beliefs drawn from the common culture. Christians who consult psychics or astrologers are not deliberately denying their faith, but they fail to see the inconsistency of their practice. Our faith calls us to trust God, even if we don't know what will happen to us today.

Christians who believe in a purely "success-oriented" faith do not see the spiritual danger of using faith as a tool for one's own ends. The Christian faith challenges us and makes demands on us; it offers us wholeness more than it offers us outward "success." The preacher who wants to draw an analogy between Baal-worship and modern idolatry must discern the ways in which the theology of the congregation is distorted, inadequate, or commingled with beliefs from the wider culture.

The historical and political situation behind Hosea 11 was the rise of Assyrian power under Tiglath-Pileser III, a military leader of extraordinary skill who expanded Assyrian territory and deported defeated people from their homelands.[7] At the time of the preaching of this oracle, some of the population of the Northern Kingdom had been deported, though Samaria had not yet fallen. The Assyrian threat was accompanied by internal chaos in Israel, resulting in social crisis. Hosea interprets these events as punishment from God (10:6; 11:5). The historical situation itself and Hosea's interpretation of it present the preacher with a twofold problem.

If this passage is preached in North American contexts, the historical situation behind it will be difficult for congregations to identify with. With the exception of recent immigrants, people in North America have never experienced anything like the total destruction caused by the Assyrian siege of Israel and its capital Samaria.[8] Following the terrorist attacks of September 11, 2001, people in North America have experienced awful destruction, senseless violence, and fear resulting from that event; but we still have a stable government and have not been defeated militarily. The events of September 11 give a new perspective to our study of the prophets, because we in North America can empathize to some extent with the grief, fear, and loss that must have affected the people of Israel under the Assyrian siege. Nevertheless, the situation in Hosea's time was much more severe than what we have experienced in North America in the twenty-first century.

We also know something of the destruction of forces of nature: floods, hurricanes, earthquakes, fires, and tornadoes. If the preacher wants to use Hosea 11 to speak to situations of suffering (an appropriate use of this chapter), the analogies must be carefully drawn, avoiding the implication that we can fully comprehend or empathize with the situation of the people of the Northern Kingdom of Israel.

The second problem confronting the preacher is the interpretation of the Assyrian military threat as punishment from God. The preacher must navigate between two false assumptions: that tragic events *never* contain an element of judgment or that *every* bad thing that happens is a punishment from God. Following the terrorist attacks of September 11, some preachers tried to exploit the attacks to further their own agendas. Such attempts are reprehensible. Nevertheless, at some point in the process, perhaps after a resolution of the wider conflict, the whole event could serve as a motivation for American soul-searching. The preacher must use theological discernment to determine how God acts through nature and history to judge human sin and to see how our sins sometimes bring their own judgment.

Despite these challenges to preaching from Hosea 11, it remains an important source for the church's proclamation. Every text presents problems for preaching. Hosea 11 is a remarkable literary and theological achievement in which the prophet reflects deeply on God's struggle to love wayward Israel, and, by extension, the church. Hosea speaks on behalf of a God who feels the human emotions of hurt and anger but chooses to rise above them to show love and compassion. Hosea's God does not take sin lightly. God does punish, but only as a corrective to reprove Israel. God's love is not naive or sentimental, but dependable, courageous, and healing. The depiction of God's struggle to love is poignant and makes Hosea's God accessible, without diminishing God's power and transcendence.

Sermon

"Will God Give Up on Us?"

I have always thought that preachers should find sermon illustrations wherever they can. Preachers never quite know where they will find something that will help them make a point in a sermon. A few years ago, I discovered a theological idea in an unusual place. I didn't expect to find one there, and you might be surprised at where I found it. This sermon illustration was written on the wall in a restroom. We are used to seeing ideas of all sorts written on the walls of restrooms, and most of them don't preach very well. But this restroom was in a theological seminary. It shows that even people in seminary write things on restroom walls, but it's just a little different from what's written in other places. On the washroom wall of this theological seminary, someone had written, "I like to sin, God likes to forgive sin—What a deal!" (The alert reader will recognize the influence of Heinrich Heine on the washroom philosopher!)

This washroom philosopher summarizes an image of God that sometimes forms in our heads. We may not have carefully thought this image out; it may have just crept slowly into our thinking. We picture God as a kindly, indulgent deity who doesn't take sin very seriously. This God winks at our transgressions, a jolly Santa Claus who never musters enough anger to give us any reason to expect judgment. The washroom philosopher believes in a God who cheerfully overlooks our sins and demands nothing from us.

This image of God can even be reinforced at church. We hear that God loves us unconditionally, that God is there for us, that "There is a Wideness in God's Mercy." If we hear that often enough, we might just settle into the belief that God is a warm, fuzzy teddy bear. That sounds like the kind of God the washroom philosopher believed in.

The feel-good God of the washroom philosopher is not the only way we see God. Sometimes, we see God very differently, one might even say as the opposite kind of God. A friend from college came to me once. He was not a churchgoer, but he wanted me to pray for his gravely ill father. He wanted me to pray because, in his words, "If I pray, God would be too busy looking through the past-due accounts to get to the prayer." My friend understood something that the washroom philosopher did not. He understood that God takes sin seriously. But my friend went too far the other way. He saw God as so angry, so judgmental, so demanding that even in a crisis, when my friend desperately needed comfort, God wouldn't listen, even to a heartfelt prayer for his father.

We hear things in church that lead us to believe in this kind of God. We remember our Puritan heritage, with sermons such as Jonathan Edwards's "Sinners in the Hands of an Angry God." Perhaps certain stories from the Bible, such as the saga of Sodom and Gomorrah, have helped to plant this view of God in our heads.

So between my friend and the washroom philosopher, we have two images of God. One image is of God as laid back, blowing off our sins as no big deal. The other is of a stern God who demands something of us but never shows compassion, even in our deepest needs.

We bounce back and forth between these two images of God, perhaps without even stopping to think about it. Surely, we see God through the eyes of the washroom philosopher when we let ourselves get away with something because "No one will ever know." Whenever we assume that God is on our side, that our success is God's top priority, that our money and our time belong to us and not to God, and whenever we ignore the needs of the poor, we are agreeing with the washroom philosopher that God makes no demands on us.

Other times, our image of God is closer to that of my friend. We see God as unapproachable, angry with us for our sins, and unmoved by our troubles. This image of God lies behind our inability to feel forgiven, our belief that our problems are too small for God to care about, and our feeling that God is distant, gone from our lives.

Sometimes we believe in the god of the washroom philosopher, and sometimes we believe in the god of my friend. Each of these images of God hides the real God from us. Each one, if we try to live by it, can hurt our faith. The god of the washroom philosopher does not push us to grow in our faith, to make sacrifices, to see beyond our own needs. The god of my friend does not reach out to us in love. Rather, my friend's god leaves us in our guilt, with no place to turn.

Hosea preached to people who had distorted images of God as well. At first, Hosea's congregation thought God would overlook their sins. They believed in the god of the washroom philosopher. Things were going well under Jeroboam II, and prosperity surely meant that God was on their side. Then tragedy struck. The Assyrians defeated them in a war and carried them into captivity. All of a sudden they believed in my friend's god. They believed God didn't care for them anymore.

Hosea tells them and us about another way of understanding God. Hosea tells us about a God who is a loving parent. This God looks back on Israel's history the way a parent looks back on the highlights of a child's growing-up years. Parts of this passage are difficult to translate, but Hosea gives rich word-pictures of a parent's tender care. The parent teaches the child to walk. Part of verse 4 may refer to a mother holding a child to her body to nurse him. As a parent remembers such things, so God remembers bringing Israel out of slavery from Egypt, and leading them through the wilderness.

Now Israel has turned away from God, and God's heart is broken. Hosea knew something like what Luke knew: that when the prodigal son goes to the far country, the Father will run out to greet him when he returns. Hosea points us toward Paul's words that while we were yet sinners, Christ died for us.

For Hosea to compare God to a loving parent gives us a deeper understanding of God. If God is a judge—and we need to hear that sometimes—Hosea tells us that God is not only a judge. For Hosea, God might be like the mother who comes to visit her son in prison after the judgment has been rendered. She shudders when the steel doors clang behind her. She walks down the long corridor to the visiting area, all the while remembering her son's first words, his first steps, his first scraped knee. She may not like what her son has done; but when she sees him in the visiting area, she swallows the lump in her throat, smiles, and hugs him, because he is her son.

Just as such a mother will not give up on her son, so God will not give up on us. For all of the problems we face in translating this passage, one thing comes through clearly. God is tempted to leave us in our sins, to turn away from us, to stop trying to help us; but our Heavenly Parent refuses to do so. God's heart rages, but God won't give up on us. God's heart breaks for our sin; but God is God, not a human being.

God may have been tempted to give up on the church when it supported slavery and segregation, but God didn't give up. God may be tempted to give up on the church when it bickers over small things, but God doesn't give up. God may be tempted to give up on us when we are greedy or when we don't speak out for what is right or when our tempers hurt our families or when we don't care enough about others. However often we have disappointed God, and however far we have strayed, God will love us still. Even if we don't understand that love, it is still there for us. Even if we take advantage of that love, it is still there for us. God keeps loving us until it finally sinks in, and we are changed.

SERMON
"Hoping in the Love of God"
Ann I. Hoch

It is a hopeless predicament. Relationships between nations and their leaders are broken at best and nonexistent at worst. No one honors previous treaties, and promises of averting violence are nothing but empty rhetoric. Leaders are swayed by money and by prevailing popular opinion. Military powers stockpile weapons. The economy is bad for the rich, and worse for the poor. Pathetic describes a lot of life. Honesty is the exception, and distrust is the rule.

Moreover, the political situation mirrors the religious one. People—at the top, at the bottom, and in between—don't know where the future lies or where to turn for guidance. So everyone grasps for the nearest "quick fix" and abandons any long-established traditions or loyalties. Even the "religious" no longer hold out hope in God—whose promises they now view with cynicism, if they hold out for God at all.

Then onto the scene arrives Hosea. Hosea, with the gift or curse of prophecy, assesses the predicament of the day and sees doom at the next turn in the road. He recognizes moral decay in the public sphere, but he sees behind that to the abandonment of faith on the religious front. He wants to call Israel's attention to the divine desire for relationship between God and humanity, so he uses familiar metaphors to do just that.

In earlier chapters, Hosea employs the metaphor of an adulterous wife for Israel's immorality and infidelity in juxtaposition to God as a faithful and loving husband. Now the metaphor shifts. Israel's faithlessness is depicted by a wayward and rebellious child. This ungrateful brat is set in contrast to God, the devoted and loving parent.

Whichever side of a child's rebellion you may have been on, all of us know a bit about rebellion. We have seen it associated with various movements in civil rights, protests against wars, musical crazes, expressions of self, and in loyalties to hairstyles, clothes, and various body disfigurements–I mean, art. Some of us know of waywardness that manifests itself in unwillingness to commit to anything but "to want what I want, when I want it."

Every generation knows the struggle of parent-child relations. Yet here is the irony: parental love of a child is a profound and primeval bond that crosses all times and places. Hosea, like all of us, knows this. So he uses the parent-child relationship as a metaphor for God's relationship to Israel. And what poignant and passionate words Hosea has God utter:

> When Israel was a child, I loved him
> and out of Egypt I called my son.
> The more I called them,
>   the more they went from me;
> they kept sacrificing to the Baals,
>   and offering incense to idols.
> Yet it was I who taught Ephraim to walk,
>   I took them up in my arms;
> but they did not know that I healed them.
> I led them with cords of human kindness,
>   with bands of love.
> I was to them like those
>   who lift infants to their cheeks.
>   I bent down to them and fed them.
> (Hosea 11:1–4)

Hosea stakes Israel's theological hope for the present and the future on God's parental love in the past. You see, by introducing the image of parental love and childlike disobedience, Hosea can place in tension the protection and the punishment of the child. Both integrally belong to a parent's desire to nurture a child for life.⁹ Because of Israel's disobedience, all manner of catastrophes are presently happening. Punishment for sin and failure to obey God is being meted out to this child.

The present punishment, however, is not all that it could be. In fact, Hosea hangs onto hope for the future and claims that Israel will get a new start. Israel gets sent to "time out," even if "time out" is in Assyria or Egypt. In other words, Israel gets sent back to "Go," or to the beginning site of God's calling of this chosen people. Israel's history in exodus, wilderness, and homeland is the paradigm for Hosea's prophecy of redemption.¹⁰

The child, to be sure, will be punished; but the severity of the punishment does not correspond to the extent of the child's rebellion and disobedience. Why? Because God is God and does not judge and sentence wrongdoing like human beings do. God's heart may be broken over the straying child, but God's love yearns for the child to turn around and be reconciled:

> How can I give you up, Ephraim?
> surrender you, O Israel?
> How can I make you like Admah?
> treat you like Zeboiim?
> My heart has turned itself against me;
> my compassion grows completely warm.
> I will not execute my burning anger;
> I will not again destroy Ephraim.
> For God am I, not man,
> the Holy One in your midst.
> I will not come to consume.
>   (Hosea 11:8–9)¹¹

Can't you hear the agony, the pleading? The words sound like the laments we hear from Job, Jeremiah, and even Jesus; but God addresses the words here to human beings. The assurance that comes is that God's wrath against Israel's rejection and abandonment of God will not bring the relationship to an end. God's love is a greater power than God's anger.

Ultimately, Hosea describes a future in which the child Israel recognizes God as the loving parent and is restored to a faithful relationship. God takes Israel back home. As one writer puts it, "Hosea trusted in the grace of God to make this relationship of faithful obedience possible. The question in his mind was whether the people would respond. But even on this question, Hosea was hopeful."[12]

Again, it is a hopeless predicament. Relationships between nations and their leaders are broken at best and nonexistent at worst. No one is honoring previous treaties, and promises of averting violence are nothing but empty rhetoric. Leaders are swayed by money and by prevailing popular opinion. Military powers stockpile weapons, and the economy is bad for the rich and worse for the poor. Pathetic describes a lot of life. Honesty is the exception, and distrust is the rule.

Moreover, the political situation mirrors the religious one. People–at the top, at the bottom, and in between–don't know where the future lies or where to turn for guidance. So everyone grasps for the nearest "quick fix" and abandons any long-established traditions or loyalties. Even the "religious"–if they hold out for God at all–no longer hold out hope in the God whose promises they now view with cynicism. And onto the scene arrives...? Who arrives on our scene to remind us of our disobedience and faithlessness? Who points to the love of God as our only hope in the future?

After September 11, 2001, for a brief time, churches in the United States experienced a drastic resurgence in attendance. Some predicted that national and international events would prompt a religious revival in the land. Alas, after the shock wore off, business got back to its routines. Fear and uncertainty no longer drove masses of people to their knees. Even many "religious" people no longer felt the urgency to turn to God. Instead, they called upon other powers to make things right. Faithlessness encompasses more than simply not going to church. It is rooted in "doubt of God's providential care."[13]

Phil Kenneson writes, "...if we desire to cooperate with God's desire to cultivate faithfulness in our lives, we will have to do so in the midst of a culture that traffics in the impermanent and the fleeting...If God is to cultivate faithfulness in our lives, Christians," he says, "will need to focus on those resources God has provided us for so doing."[14] Among those resources are the telling and retelling of stories from the past and present that celebrate God's loving and abiding presence—a presence that is always faithful and that asks us to respond with faithfulness. One practice that helps to promote faithfulness is making and keeping promises "because we worship a promise-making and promise-keeping God who has called us to do the same as a witness, even if an imperfect one, to God's own faithfulness."[15] Further, we can learn to tell the truth, first acknowledging the truth about our own shortcomings, and then recognizing that the truth in love lies beyond ourselves. Indeed, it is at the heart of faith.

This is the task the church has—to speak to the heirs of God's covenantal relationship with Israel. And the message, in the words of Peter Gomes, is this:

> God's immediate and ultimate relationship to the world is one not of power or of indifference but of affection: For God so loved the world. God's power is subordinate to his love. The world is subordinate to his love. The world is a place that is beloved of God. Like creation it is good, although terrible things happen in it for it is not perfect, it is not without pain, and the price of our freedom is to learn to cope with a world of ambiguity and danger, pain, joy, and opportunity. Through all of that God relates to us out of his love for us...
>
> God's love is God's ultimate action and it is given human form in Jesus Christ, and if God can invest himself and his love in the unlikely form of a man born of woman, who suffered as we suffer and died as we shall die, dare we invest less in humanity than God?[16]

More importantly, I would add, dare we not invest in faithfulness and love in the One who has more faith in us than we have in ourselves and who has always loved us and always will? With Hosea, do we trust in the grace of God to make a relationship of faithful obedience possible? If so, how will we respond?

CHAPTER 4

Introduction to Amos

The prophet Amos was active around the same time as Hosea, although Amos was slightly earlier, by most accounts. From the evidence we have in his book, his ministry was much shorter than Hosea's, at most no more than a year in duration. Amos prophesied during the reign of Jeroboam II and so conducted his ministry during the years of prosperity of the Northern Kingdom.[1] One of Amos's primary concerns was that the prosperity was concentrated in the hands of a few, with the poor being left out. In forceful and sometimes even rude language, Amos announced YHWH's pending judgment on Israel.

Although by the end of Hosea's ministry the people could begin to see the serious military and political threat posed by Assyria, during Amos's ministry the people apparently were comfortable and complacent. The burden of Amos's ministry was to preach to these complacent and prosperous people that their success did not indicate YHWH's favor. YHWH judged how they handled—and how they shared—that prosperity. Without the obvious threat of Assyria to point to, Amos had to rely on the efficacy of his words to persuade the people that their neglect of the underclass had aroused YHWH's wrath.

Scholars see in the book of Amos a decisive shift in the nature of prophecy in the Old Testament. The earlier prophets had condemned the sins of individual persons, such as David (Nathan) or Ahab (Elijah). Even though lines of continuity connect Amos and these earlier prophets, Amos begins the practice of directing oracles of judgment against the entire nation.[2] Amos goes so far as to say that YHWH will destroy the nation of Israel. Needless to say, Amos's words were not popular. And in the sense of producing the desired response, they were not successful. His words, however, help us interpret the power and sovereignty of God. They communicate God's judgment on how the community of faith handles issues of economic and social justice.

The book of Amos can be divided into 3 sections: chapters 1–2, chapters 3–6, and chapters 7–9. Chapters 1–2 are oracles against foreign nations, ending with oracles against Judah and Israel. Chapters 3–6 are oracles to Israel, and 7–9 is the book of Amos's visions. Unlike the book of Hosea, in which oracles of judgment were interspersed with assurances of God's grace, Amos preached a nearly unrelenting word of judgment. YHWH had acted graciously in Israel's past, but now God comes to punish. Only at the end of the book, in chapter 9, is there a clear promise of grace for the future, although chapter 5 calls for repentance, which might stay God's judgment.

Scholars are divided about the way in which the book of Amos took its final form. A likely scenario is that only part of the book derives from the prophet Amos himself. In all probability, those parts are the oracles that announced total destruction of Israel, with no possibility of repentance (e.g., 4:1–3). After the fall of Samaria, an event that vindicated Amos's proclamation, Amos's words were then taken to the Southern Kingdom of Judah. There Amos's message was used to warn the people of Judah and to motivate them to repent. The oracles that offer an opportunity to repent were added (e.g., 5:4–7). Finally, the oracle of salvation in 9:11–15 was added during the exile to offer hope to the defeated people.[3] Perhaps it is enough to say that Amos's primary message was of judgment, with a few exhortations to repent and a closing oracle of grace and salvation.

Chapters 1–2

The first two verses of Amos give us valuable, but somewhat cryptic, information about Amos and the book. The superscription, contained in the first verse, identifies Amos as a "shepherd" from Tekoa. Scholars have tried mightily to determine Amos's social location and exact occupation. In all likelihood, Amos was a well-educated businessman from the Southern Kingdom of Judah, who went north to preach in Israel.[4] As discussed above, the reigns of Jeroboam and Uzziah were times of relative prosperity and political success for Israel and Judah.

Verse 2 sets the tone for the book and serves as a kind of thesis sentence. Amos compares YHWH to a lion who "roars" from Zion. The blast from YHWH's roar withers grass and causes the top of Mt. Carmel to dry up. This ferocious image for God sets Amos's agenda early in the book. God is powerful and fearsome. God is sovereign over human affairs (hence the reference to the city of Jerusalem), and over the realm of nature (as indicated by the destruction of pasturelands and mountains).

In Amos 1:3 to 2:3, that fierce nature of God manifests itself in oracles of judgment against countries bordering Israel and Judah. This part of Amos is usually labeled "the oracles against the nations." Similar sections appear in Isaiah 13–23; Jeremiah 46–51; Ezekiel 25–32; and Zephaniah 2:4–15; as well as in the books of Obadiah and Nahum. These oracles announce YHWH's judgment against these countries for what we would call human rights violations. In acts of war or other aggression, these countries have acted cruelly. Damascus has committed egregious acts of violence during war ("threshed Gilead"). Amon has tortured and mutilated pregnant women. Moab has violated the bodies of the dead.

Although these oracles might not serve well as sermon texts by themselves, they could be used within sermons to make two important points. First, God's righteous anger is not capricious. God becomes angry when people are hurt, abused, tortured, and exploited. Secondly, even though pastors proclaim the words of the prophets within the church, the church itself is called to proclaim God's judgment beyond its own walls. The church has a warrant from these oracles against the nations in Amos to announce God's judgment wherever atrocities are committed. God is sovereign over all people. God judges war crimes, brutality, and heinous acts against human dignity.

The last two oracles are against Judah and Israel. Commentators have frequently remarked about the rhetorical effect of presenting the oracles against the nations first and then dropping a bombshell by finishing with oracles against Judah and Israel. With each passing oracle against a nation the hearer or reader is pulled into deeper agreement with the prophet. The people of Judah and Israel wanted to hear God's judgment pronounced against their bitter enemies. Suddenly, though, the spotlight is pointed at God's chosen people themselves. God judges them as well as their enemies.[5]

The oracle against Judah differs somewhat from the other accusations. The other oracles list specific actions the nations have taken. The oracle against Judah speaks in generalities. The people of Judah have rejected the Torah of YHWH and failed to obey YHWH's statutes. The exact ways in which the people have done this is not given. YHWH's Torah ("Torah" can be translated "law," "teaching," or "instruction") was a gift given to the people to aid in building community and to provide a basis for an ethical response to God's grace shown in the exodus event. If the people of Judah "rejected" this instruction, they denied, in a sense, their own identity.

The oracle against Israel accuses that nation of abusing the poor. The memorable phrase used in this passage is that they "trample the head of the poor into the dust of the earth" (2:7a). Their treatment of the poor is greedy, callous, and arrogant. Specifically, people are sold into slavery for the price of a pair of sandals (2:6); the poor are denied access to the courts (2:7b); men sexually exploit domestic help (2:7c); and collateral for debts is shown off as a kind of trophy (2:8, cf. Ex. 22:26–27).[6]

Taken together, the two oracles against Judah and Israel suggest two temptations to which the church can succumb. The church is always in danger of losing sight of its identity. The church forgets that it is a community called by God to bear witness in the world to God's power and grace. The church can forget its identity by becoming a social club or by focusing only on its own members without reaching out to others. The second temptation to which the church can succumb is to neglect its duty to advocate for, and take care of, the poor and marginalized.

Chapters 3—6

This section of Amos contains oracles announcing YHWH's judgment against Israel. This part of the book alternates between oracles that threaten Israel with utter destruction, with no provision for repentance, and oracles that call for the people to repent. As discussed above, some commentators see this difference stemming from the work of editors who included later oracles alongside Amos's own preaching.

Chapter 3 begins with a declaration of YHWH's right to punish Israel. YHWH brought the Hebrew slaves out of Egypt, formed them into a community, and established a unique and intimate relationship with them (3:1-2). As an exercise of YHWH's sovereignty, YHWH can punish the people and end the relationship. Verses 3:3-8 are a series of questions that Amos uses to defend his preaching ministry. Each question is designed to elicit an obvious answer of "no" (e.g., "Does a bird fall into a trap if there is no trap?" The obvious answer is no). The conclusion, then, is that if YHWH is going to act, surely YHWH will send a prophet to interpret those actions.

Verses 4:6-11 list the ways in which YHWH has attempted to get the people's attention. YHWH has used famine, drought, plant diseases, locust plagues, illness, and military setbacks to communicate divine anger to the people. None of those strategies worked, so YHWH has seemingly no choice but to act drastically to destroy Israel. Israel's original mission was to be a kingdom of priests, through whom all the families of the world would be blessed (Gen. 12:1-3). Amos does not say that YHWH will start over, but presumably, the original desire to bless all the families of the earth has not been abandoned.

The contemporary preacher could use this material to proclaim God's actions to create and form the church. The material can also interpret the church's mission of witnessing to God's character, grace, and power in the world. Contemporary readers may not accept that every drought or disaster is God's direct action to punish, but we can still affirm that God works through events to communicate to us. As one of my church members put it, God does not necessarily cause every event, but perhaps God "takes advantage" of what happens to get through to us.[7]

Having established YHWH's right to punish Israel, and Amos's authority to proclaim and interpret that punishment, this section of Amos offers several oracles announcing that punishment. Verses 3:12–15 declare the severity of God's judgment against Israel. The religious institutions and luxurious homes of the wealthy (perhaps an example of economic stratification) will fall. The destruction will be as devastating as a lion attacking a defenseless sheep, with only bits of the poor animal left behind. Verses 5:1–5 tell of YHWH's utter destruction of Israel, with no promised future beyond the destruction and, apparently, no hope that repentance can prevent the judgment. Such oracles must be used carefully in contemporary Christian preaching. These oracles remind us of God's power over us, God's disappointment and frustration with our failure, the reality of God's judgment, and the potential that God could choose to work outside the church to accomplish the divine ends. These oracles remind the church that it exists for God's purposes and not its own.

Verses 4:1–5 contain two oracles that employ a rhetorical strategy that contemporary Christian preachers would likely reject. Both oracles use mockery and insult to make their point. Amos refers to the wives of prominent men in the area of Bashan as pampered "cows." He then mocks their words in the last part of verse 1. The oracle closes with the threat that these well-to-do, comfortable women will be led away in a degrading, humiliating way. The second oracle (4:4–5) is a parody of a call to worship. Instead of the expected "Come to Bethel and worship," we read, "Come to Bethel–and transgress." As the oracle concludes, we read that this worship pleases only the worshiper, not YHWH ("for so you love to do"). Used carefully and with appropriate humor and pastoral sensitivity, these oracles can help the preacher make points about the church's neglect of the poor (which was the sin of the women of Bashan), and the temptation to self-absorption in our worship.

The brief oracle in 5:14–15 contains the only real justification for contemporary proclamation of judgment. These two verses call Israel to repentance. The form of this repentance is the seeking of good and the establishment of justice. (For a discussion of justice in Amos, see the exegesis on 5:18-24 on pages 64-66.)[8]

Chapter 6 is a grim pronouncement condemning the comfort and arrogance of the elite in Israelite society. The oracle describes several examples of indulgence. The rich and powerful are "at ease" (v. 1). They seek comfort and eat choice food (v. 4). They engage in merriment and enjoy fine wine (vv. 5-6). The description actually sounds much like what we today would call the "good life." The prophet condemns the leaders not merely for enjoying life, but because they have perverted justice and righteousness (v. 12). YHWH will punish Israel through the Assyrian army (v. 14). The self-indulgent leaders will be the "first" ones taken into exile. The passage provides the careful preacher with insights into the indulgences of contemporary North American society. Many covet gas-guzzling luxury cars. We are so well fed that obesity has become a serious problem. The prophet does not condemn the enjoyment of good food or the drinking of alcohol. The prophet condemns the overindulgence of those who do not care for the hunger and oppression of others. The gap between the rich and the poor in the United States has grown wider in recent years. More people are slipping into poverty. The prophet admonishes those who enjoy their excess while others barely survive.

Chapters 7–9

Beginning in chapter 7, Amos reports a series of visions. Dreams and visions as a means of revelation from God have a long history in the Old Testament. In Genesis 20, Abimelech has a dream that reveals Abraham's deception concerning Sarah. Joseph, of course, had his own dreams and interpreted the dreams of others. Zechariah and Daniel had visions, but those books were written after Amos. The first verse of the book of Amos identifies the contents of the book as the "words of Amos,...which he *saw*." Dreams and visions were not always considered reliable means of revelation in the Old Testament. Amos brings his message as an outsider to the religious establishment, and so appeals to a marginally accepted means of revelation to substantiate his message. Perhaps, when the established clergy are not open to God's sometimes disturbing and sometimes challenging word, God finds other means of getting the word through.

The first two of these visions relate how Amos convinced the Lord God to spare Israel from destruction. In the first vision, the Lord God is "forming locusts" to unleash them in a plague. If not for the devastation of locusts, the scene might be somewhat humorous: The Lord God sitting in a workshop "forming" locusts. (The Hebrew word for "forming" is the same word used in Genesis 2 for forming the man.) Amos pleads on "Jacob's" behalf, and the Lord God relents of the punishment. In the second vision (vv. 4–6), the Lord God intends to unleash a "shower of fire." This shower of fire is awesome enough to evaporate the "great deep," the primal waters themselves. Again, Amos pleads with the Lord God, who relents of the punishment.

These two short passages do much to redeem Amos in the reader's eyes as they teach us about the pastoral side of the great prophet. Amos tries in these two vision reports to convince the Lord God to turn back the punishment and give Israel a second chance. Amos takes no perverse pleasure in announcing YHWH's judgment on Israel. If it were up to Amos, YHWH would spare Israel and give the people the opportunity to repent. When preachers feel led to preach judgment, we must do so with humility and discipline.

The third vision, in 7:7–9, is cryptic and difficult to translate. The common translation (still offered by NRSV) is that YHWH holds a "plumb line" up to Israel and determines that Israel cannot be repaired (as a wall that is too warped cannot be) and so must be destroyed. Some recent commentators have called that translation into question.[9] In any case, the point of the third vision seems to be that in YHWH's estimation, the punishment can no longer be averted. Israel is beyond hope; YHWH has no choice. After Amos has persuaded YHWH twice to avert the punishment, YHWH decides that the only course of action is to destroy Israel.

The passage in 8:11–12 is a brief and often overlooked oracle that threatens a famine of "hearing the words of the

LORD." It is significant that this oracle comes after several other oracles (throughout the book) that threaten physical destruction, and after 8:9-10 that threatens cosmic chaos. This oracle suggests that an even more devastating punishment would be the absence of the word of God. Perhaps physical deprivation is even more difficult to bear if it cannot be interpreted. Spiritual alienation is a deeper, more awful punishment than physical destruction.

In 9:8b, a significant change occurs in the book of Amos. Just after the book announces in 8a that "the sinful kingdom" will be destroyed from the face of the earth, in 8b, the threat is qualified, "except that I will not utterly destroy the house of Jacob, says the LORD." In 9:9-10, the oracle describes how God will remove all of the sinners from Israel. Presumably, only just and righteous people will remain. Once the sinners have been purged, God will again rebuild. As suggested above, this oracle (especially vv. 11-15, which refer to the raising of the booth of David) likely originated during the Babylonian exile among the dispersed Judeans.

The clear word of grace comes only at the end of the book of Amos. Even though this word of grace almost certainly did not come from the lips or pen of Amos himself, in certain ways it fits here at the end of the book. The book of Amos begins with a declaration that YHWH's roar will wither the pastures and dry up the top of a mountain. God's judgment will wreak havoc on nature. Here at the end, YHWH's grace will create abundance in nature. The land will be so fertile that the crops can be harvested as soon as they are planted. The mountains will drip with an overflow of wine. Whereas YHWH had once tried to get the people's attention through drought and famine (4:6-10), YHWH will now provide flourishing gardens and vineyards.

Just as Amos did not offer the theological insights about the root causes of the people's sins (as Hosea did), so Amos's closing oracle does not tell about God acting to heal the deep-rooted sin and rebellion of the people. Verses 9-10 seem to imply that if "the sinners" are removed, the rest of the people will be faithful and obedient, acting with justice and righteousness. Nevertheless, this oracle demonstrates that God's gracious favor has the last word. The editors of Amos have produced a book that gets our attention by its fierce portrayal of God's anger and judgment, but that closes with the assurance that God's grace always follows that judgment.

Theological Reflection on Preaching Amos

In many ways, Amos is very different from Hosea. Some of the differences make Amos somewhat less attractive to us than Hosea. Hosea exposed a real vulnerability in God, portraying a God who felt genuine pain and anguish over the people's sin (chapters 1–3; 6:4; chapter 11). In Amos, God comes in judgment, showing no vulnerability. The emphasis in Amos is on the sovereignty of God over nature and history. The nation of Israel has failed to live out the justice and righteousness that God expects, and so God will destroy the nation. Although, at first glance, such a message does not appear to be particularly edifying, Amos's words have profound significance for the contemporary church. If we interpret Amos within the context of the whole canon of scripture (where God's second chances are more clearly stated), we can appropriate Amos's passionate concern for the poor and exploited along with his unwavering conviction about God's sovereignty into our preaching.

Three important theological convictions underlie the book of Amos. These convictions both serve as the warrant for the oracles of judgment, and constitute the affirmation of God's grace outside of 9:11–15 (which may be a later addition). The first of these convictions is that God is the sovereign creator of the world. Hymns often contain significant theology. Passages 4:13; 5:8–9; and 9:5–6 are hymn fragments inserted into the final form of the book of Amos. These hymns celebrate God's creation of the world and God's authority over nature.

The second conviction is that God called the people of Israel as a special community with a unique relationship to God and to the rest of humanity. Verses 9:7–8 announce this special relationship and Israel's failure to live up to its requirements.

The third conviction is that God cares deeply about the poor and exploited. Israel's most significant failure as a people is that they have not practiced justice and righteousness on behalf of society's marginalized people.[10] Amos understands justice and righteousness as Israel's proper response to God's call of Israel into special relationship. Amos forcefully states his accusations of injustice in 2:6–8. Israel's rich and powerful mistreat the poor by selling them into slavery. The law courts are not fair. Lenders show off their "trophies" taken from debtors. Stated positively, justice and righteousness include fair access to goods and services, equality before the law, and respect for the dignity of all people. Each of these convictions is also an example of God's grace–acting to create the world, calling Israel to be a special people, and advocating for the poor are all manifestations of God's gracious providence.

These acts of grace are in the past (with care for the poor continuing into the present). The only word of future grace for the people of Israel as a community comes in 9:11–15. Even in this book, with its fierce denunciations of Israel, God's grace comes through, but the emphasis is on God's power and sovereignty.

Perhaps Amos's most important contribution to contemporary Christian preaching is the book's attention to the large issues of social justice. The book gives preachers material to address current examples of torture (1:13), injustice in the courts (5:15), sexual harassment (2:7c), international human rights abuses (1:9), and the plight of the poor (2:6–8). Amos does not prescribe specific social policies (e.g., he does not advocate a particular economic system). Amos does announce God's expectation that all people will be respected and treated fairly, will be taken care of, and will have the opportunity to contribute to the community. If Amos's words seem harsh, they likely reflect God's frustration over how short the church and society fall in fulfilling these expectations.

CHAPTER 5

Amos 5:18–24

Exegesis

This passage is frightening. Its portrayal of God leaves us breathless and drained. Its very ferocity and uncompromising judgment compel us to hear it, despite how uncomfortable it makes us. Two of the convictions of this passage—that God is dangerous and that God can be repulsed by worship—crack wide open any sense of complacency about our faith. God takes justice and righteousness so seriously that God can act like a wild animal or turn away from the people's prayers and songs.

Amos 5:18–24 is likely a collection of individual units that now form a single passage. In just a few verses the passage covers an amazing panoply of ideas, often expressed in evocative metaphors. The first subunit of the passage covers verses 18–20. It begins and ends with the "day of YHWH." Sandwiched between the two sayings about the day of YHWH is a skillful, but disturbing, simile about God's judgment.

In verses 18 and 20, Amos challenges the people's expectations that the day of YHWH will be a victorious celebration. The day of YHWH formed part of the national faith in YHWH. The Israelite populace apparently expected the day of YHWH to be a time when God intervened to deliver the nation from its enemies. It involved part historical and part eschatological hopes. Amos turned the people's expectation on its head. YHWH was not coming to intervene decisively for the people, but in an act of judgment against the people! The day of YHWH might be a time of punishment for Israel's enemies, but it would be even more a time of punishment for Israel.

Verse 19 is a skillfully written vignette that paints a foreboding picture of God. With just a few words, the author creates a dramatic scene. A man flees from a lion, but runs into a bear. With just a little imagination, we can visualize the wide-eyed panic on the man's face, hear his heart pounding in his chest, and imagine his terrified gasps for air. As he reaches his house, we can hear the long, slow expulsion of air as the feeling of relief washes over him.

Whether the verse describes one episode (the man escapes from both the lion and the bear, but a snake bites him), or two episodes (one man is killed by the bear and another by a snake), the visceral effect is the same. Just as the man thinks he is safe, the real danger appears. This is an almost fiendish image of God. The fear evoked by the lion and the bear are not enough. The writer drags out the suspense, so that as the man reaches home, and safety, the snake unexpectedly appears to bite him. God is not only judging, but is doing so relentlessly, allowing no avenue of escape.

Following shortly on this devastating image of God is Amos's taunt (5:21–27) that God is repulsed by Israel's worship. The rejection of worship is complete, a triple-whammy. God will not smell the offerings, look upon them, or hear the songs. God closes off all of the divine senses to Israel's worship.

Verse 24 implies the reason for both God's feral punishment and rejection of worship: the absence of justice and righteousness in Israel's society. Justice and righteousness are parallel terms referring to basic fairness and economic equity in society. These concepts extend to the courts, business practices, and to provision of and access to services.

Verse 24 generates a powerful image. Justice rolling down like waters evokes the idea of a sudden rainstorm, bringing instant water. Righteousness is a stream that never runs dry, providing a constant, dependable supply. Justice and righteousness should be quick and long lasting.

This passage offers a sharp critique of our worship. In the simplest terms, we understand worship as our response (formal and informal, individual and collective) to God's activity and presence. Amos's words here compel us to see not only our individual actions, but also the structure of society as part of that response. The indictment in this passage is on the whole community. The business sector, the judicial system, and the social agencies were to be founded on justice. Our worship is authentic and pleasing to God when it issues in individual and collective efforts to form a more just society.

Used with care, this passage can be a powerful word in contemporary preaching. We must use care in proclaiming this passage because many people in the pews already have a morbid fear of God. People struggling with depression or addiction may especially feel unworthy of God. To preach carelessly that God rejects our worship or will attack like a wild animal would do further damage.

With this caution in mind, preachers can push congregations, communities, and even nations to take seriously God's demand for justice. The church is called to work to alleviate poverty, solve problems in our penal system, combat the neglect and abuse of the vulnerable, and improve the health of the environment. The ferocity of this passage is a goad to the church to persevere, even in the face of obstacles, in our quest to build a more just society. Although this passage is harsh, even Amos would say that, ultimately, our reason for working toward justice is not fear, but the assurance that God has acted graciously toward us.

In the sermon below I make an interpretive move. I call the church to work for justice and righteousness, but I also interpret justice and righteousness as God's will that cannot ultimately be thwarted. In light of the whole canon, I use Amos's imagery of justice and righteousness as water as an eschatological promise. The church is called to work for justice, but also to bear witness to the justice God will establish in God's reign.

SERMON

"Rain in the Forecast"

Amos 5:18–24 and 1 Peter 1:3–12

I don't recall this incident, so what you are getting is hearsay. My reliable source for this story is my parents, who told me of it several times. When I was a young lad, my family was driving on a trip and stopped at a gas station. As it happened, I spotted a bear in a cage in the gas station's parking lot. I went up to my mother and announced that I wanted to go pet the bear.

However old I was, I wasn't old enough to appreciate irony. When my mother said, "Oh yeah, that's a good thing for you to do," I took her literally and went off to pet the bear. You can tell from the fact that I still have both of my arms that I didn't make it to the bear's cage, and that the bear went unpetted. From what I have been told, however, I came pretty close. We chuckle at this story, but if I had been able to run a little faster at that age, it might not be funny at all.

Amos's view of God at the beginning of this passage is no laughing matter. Amos gives us a startling, and even frightening, view of God. God is a bear. We are used to God being lots of things: a mother comforting her children, a protective father, a sturdy rock, a shepherd. But we are not used to hearing that God is a bear.

We would find it hard to pray to a bear; a bear would not comfort us. We fear bears.

Amos wants us to feel such fear. Amos wants us to know that God is angry. Amos's first readers didn't expect an angry God. Amos is turning their expectations upside down. Amos's congregation expected a God who was on their side. They expected a day of triumph, a "day of the LORD," when God would be fully revealed, and they would rejoice. They were looking forward to that day. They longed for that day. They prayed for that day, just as we pray each week in the Lord's Prayer that God's kingdom will come. Amos warns them not to look forward to the "day of the LORD." The Lord is angry. Amos tells them that the day of the LORD will not be what they expect. They should fear the day of the LORD, because God is a bear.

In telling his congregation to fear the day of the LORD, Amos sets out three terrifying images. In the first image, Amos tells a brief story with an unhappy ending. A man is being chased by a lion. What we want to hear is how he escapes from the lion. Amos turns things around. He escapes from the lion, all right, but just as he thinks he is safe, just as he lets out a sigh of relief, just as his heart has begun to stop pounding in his chest, the giant paw and hot breath of a bear are upon him.

God is the bear. God has claws and sharp teeth. If that first image is not terrifying enough, Amos sets another scene of a man coming into his house, resting a weary hand on a wall, and then being bitten by a snake. The man is not safe even in his own house. How is that for an image of God? How many of us want to pray to God the snake?

The third terrifying image is an image of what the day of the LORD will be like. The day of the LORD, for which Amos's congregation has been hoping and praying, will be thick darkness. When I was a pastor in Staples, Texas, one morning at 5:00 a.m. all of the lights went out. I mean *all* of the lights: in our house, outside the house, all over the neighborhood. It was utterly and completely dark, with no light anywhere.

Sandra and I finally located a flashlight, so we could see in the dark, until the sun came up. A few days later, a woman in the church told me that that morning had scared her to death. She had been having eye problems and was being treated by an ophthalmologist. She woke up that day, opened her eyes, and couldn't see a thing! She thought she had gone blind. That's what the day of the LORD will be like, according to Amos—so dark you will think you have gone blind.

According to Amos, God is angry enough to attack like a bear, or angry enough to cover the earth with darkness. Why? Because God looks down and sees people who have been treated unfairly. God sees those who have been sold into slavery for the price of a pair of shoes. God sees those who have not gotten a fair shake in the courts. God is so angry that God turns away from the people's worship.

Yes, Amos claims that worship that doesn't lead to justice is not worship at all. As God looks at those who have been treated unfairly, God sees them as dry, parched ground. We all know about dry parched ground the last few weeks. The grass withers up and turns yellow and brown. It looks unnatural. Our lawns should be thick, green, and luxurious. Instead they are dry, broken, and brittle. That is how God sees the poor.

For the poor, who look like dry, parched ground and stunted crops, Amos calls for rain. Amos utters one of the most powerful lines of all scripture here: "Let justice roll down like waters, / and righteousness like an ever-flowing stream."

From the terrifying imagery earlier in the chapter, Amos now uses beautiful imagery. Justice and righteousness should be like a refreshing, life-giving shower. We don't have time to wait for justice, so let it come like a sudden shower, bathing the dry, parched ground. Let righteousness be like a stream that never runs dry. We need justice that is quick, and we need a never-ending supply.

Amos calls for a rain shower of justice to wash away the poor people's pain: the pain of unfairness, of the brutality of poverty. Amos issues a call to Israel to get involved in people's lives, to work for what is right, to fix what is broken, to return what has been taken away. Amos's call to Israel extends to the church.

We in the church are called to offer the refreshing waters of justice to those who are poor, who have been trampled underfoot by life. We are called to raise our voices to protest injustice and inequality. We in the church are called to a special kind of task. We are called to work as hard as we can, knowing that we will never solve all of the world's problems of poverty and injustice. We cannot heal all of the world's hurts by our own efforts. Nevertheless, we cannot allow our inability to do everything to keep us from doing what we can. We cannot end injustice, but we can alleviate some injustices. We cannot end poverty, but we can help the poor. We are to do all we can, knowing that we cannot do it all. Because we can never do it all, we proclaim that Amos's call for justice is more than a call. Amos's call also contains the seeds of a promise. Justice and righteousness are God's will, and ultimately nothing can stop God's will.

As the passage from 1 Peter proclaims, an inheritance awaits us, an inheritance that is undefiled and imperishable. That inheritance includes justice, when what is wrong will be set right. In the inheritance God has for us, justice—true and lasting justice—will come.

A movie of a few years ago, *The Shawshank Redemption*, contains a moving scene. Tim Robbins portrays a banker named Andy Dufresne. This banker is convicted of a crime he didn't commit. While incarcerated in Shawshank Prison, he is treated brutally. The warden exploits his accounting skills to embezzle money. Some of the other prisoners resent Andy's education and rough him up.

For twenty years Andy chips away at the wall of his cell in the hopes of making his escape. One stormy night Andy finally crawls through the hole that is now big enough. He inches his way through a sewer pipe to freedom. When he comes to the end of the pipe, he falls into the stream to which the pipe leads. Andy stands up and begins to run in the stream. He takes off his prison shirt and his undershirt and stops for a moment. He looks up and raises his arms to the sky. Surrounded by the water in the stream, and with the rain pouring over him, Andy smiles and then laughs. The rain washes away the dirt from the pipe, but it also seemingly washes away the years of injustice and brutality. The water refreshes him and dissolves the hurt and mistreatment.

The day is coming when all of us will hold our arms up to heaven and feel the waters of justice wash over us, refresh us, and cleanse us. We can name the ones who need the water of justice the most. Those who lived through slavery and segregation will hold up their hands to heaven and feel the waters of justice wash over them. Those who now live in refugee camps, with no home to go back to, will hold up their hands to heaven and feel the waters of justice wash over them. Those in Latin America who have had family members disappear and don't know what has happened to them will hold their hands up to heaven and feel the waters of justice wash over them.

Victims of discrimination, children who did not get enough to eat for their bodies and minds to develop right, the sick who don't get proper medical care because they can't pay for it, the mentally ill who are herded off into hospitals with little treatment–all will hold their hands up to heaven and feel the waters of justice wash over them. All of us who have endured injustices large or small, all of us who grieve for the plight of the poor, all who are frustrated because we can't do enough to help others, will hold our hands up to heaven and feel the waters of justice wash over us.

We need rain here in Montague County, but we need Amos's shower of justice and ever-flowing streams of righteousness even more.

Sermon

"Let Justice Roll"

William C. Turner

> Take away from me the noise of your songs;
>   I will not listen to the melody of your harps.
> But let justice roll down like waters,
>   and righteousness like an ever-flowing stream.
> (5:23–24)

Amos was an eighth-century prophet who exercised his call in the Northern Kingdom at the shrines of Dan and Bethel. When challenged by the official prophets, he claimed to be neither a prophet nor the son of a prophet, but a herdsman and a gatherer of sycamore fruit. Coming in the tradition of the seer, he was told to flee, because the land was not able to contain his words.

Get a picture of him, if you can. He did not have the appearance of one with a prophet's attire. Neither did he have the pedigree. All he knew was that God's hand was on him and that his sense of the presence and power of God did not permit him to withstand God's power. He protested with all the strength within him, not wanting the identity that went with the prophetic office.

In the eyes of many, the vocation of the prophet was not honorable, to say the least. They considered prophets to be shiftless people, little more than troublemakers. They labeled prophets misfits—persons seeking to earn a living from their oracles without contributing anything productive to the culture. The man of the Spirit *('ish haruach)* was considered to be something of a manipulator. He seduced himself into a trance, claimed questionable powers, and stirred the people into a frenzy. The priest had the duty to rid the land of these morally weak characters.

We call Amos a minor prophet because of the amount of writing credited to him. But we can hardly consider the impact and influence of his oracles minor. Throughout the centuries the words of this prophet have resounded with compelling force: "let justice roll down like waters."

What is truly outstanding about this prophet is the clarity of the ethical pronouncements. Fearlessly, uncompromisingly, he decried those who used their power and position to defraud the poor and grind the needy into the dust.

Here we see the prophetic view given in bold relief. The prophetic word does not deal with what the mighty and powerful are doing because of their strength. The prophetic word is about what God is doing in the world.

One knows what God is doing by looking at the condition of the least among the people, the wretched of the earth–those the world despises. Not the wise and prudent, not the mighty and noted ones, but those who would otherwise be ground into the dust are the ones the Lord defends. Truly, this God casts down the mighty from their thrones of power and raises the poor from the dung heap. With righteousness God judges the poor. With equity God reproves to help the meek of the earth. This is God's habit, the way God always works. Those who truly speak in the name of the Lord develop the same habit.

What this prophet shows us is the principle to distinguish between God's way and the interpretation of history favoring the powerful. What we have is the contest over how we know what God is doing in the world. We do not know the will of God from the behavior of those who are mighty, powerful, and great in the sight of men and women. Knowing the will of God requires a knowledge of God not given in the exploits of those whom the world calls great. Rather, such knowledge of God comes only through prophetic insight.

Here Amos established a sharp distinction between religious ritual and the ways of the covenant. Religion consists of an inner disposition as well as outward manners. Unfortunately, all too often the outward projection receives the most attention.

Rituals of sacrifice and worship, formal acts of going to the sacred places and singing songs, acts of piety and devotion—God's people so often use these worship practices to mask over an inward disposition in rebellion against God. This mistake produces horrendous results. We demand that God favor us. We recreate God in the worshiper's image, rather than letting God form the worshiper into God's image.

O so easily we force God to favor us—or at least that is the attempt. We believe God is present when we have done things right: held the right opinion, carried out the right liturgy, produced the right sort of music. Our "worship" procedures can offend God as much as did the sounds of the instruments and the odor of the sacrifices in the prophet's day. Or, is it possible for us to become so enamored of our forms that we usher God out if perchance the music that pleases God comes with a sound we do not prefer? The noise we consider rude and unpleasant may just be the mode God prefers—precisely because it comes from a life that is truly devoted.

Religion! Religion! Oh so easily we can use it to mask our mess. We use vestments to camouflage toxic social venom. Songs cover economic sin. Performance hides political perfidy. Rituals blot out rottenness.

We rightly shudder when we remember that less than two centuries ago our preachers proclaimed that holding slaves as property was in keeping with God's word. The church often commended slaveholders for their piety. So horrible was the hypocrisy that some slaves begged not to be sold to Christian masters. Those slaves heard reports that treatment would be far better at the hands of those who made no profession of faith in Christ. No injustice is worse than to have it preceded by reading from the Holy Writ. Similar forms of injustice live today under the horrid harbor of literal reading of texts. We still construe texts as positive divine sanction of our exploitation of power against the weak.

Injustice is inscribed in patterns that are equally pernicious through some of the high-sounding, high-styled celebrities of popular religious culture. How are the perversions of Amos's day different from those of ours? We see preachers fleece the flock for more cars than one person can drive, demand personal jets to travel in the name of a humble carpenter, and build mansions in honor of the preacher who had nowhere to lay his head. We continue to sell the poor for a pair of shoes when workers are laid off, while the executive who sends them away with the pink slip receives a bonus. Rotten food and sloppy witness result when we substitute the worship of personal appetite for the worship of the true and living God.

Religion! Religion! Which choir is singing? Which songs do I like? Which preacher is preaching? Is the decor coordinated? Which club is in charge?

What horrible exchanges we make if we are not duly chastised by this prophetic word. The prophetic word breaks the silence, pierces our private spheres, and penetrates into our privileged spaces. It descends upon us and invades our sensibilities, even as did this rustic prophet who showed up in the cultural center—at the shrine where the priest presumed to have custody.

The prophetic word offers no way rightly to confuse rituals and formal pronouncements with radical obedience to God. The prophetic priority was on justice, mercy, and compassion. The people were told to take away the sound of their instruments and the noise most often associated with the worship of God. Living in a disobedient state, evidenced by their oppression of the poor, they should not expect God to hear them. Indeed, what they offered as praise to God was little more than an offensive and distracting noise.

Religion is no substitute for righteousness, nor is piety the replacement for covenant loyalty and obedience to God. Religious sounds not accompanied by sound faith are no less than annoying. The unfaithful waited for the religious feast days to end so they could resume their economic oppression of the poor and the needy. Rather than looking upon the weak ones as those whom they could bless to show forth the love of God, they took the weakness as a sign of lack of God's favor and their chance to gain an advantage.

This is truly a word that spoke to the heart of the African American Church. There may be no word that was dearer to the premier prophet of the twentieth century—Martin Luther King Jr. No person spoke with more force and authority in challenge of American docetism—our separating the faith from what matters.

Justice has to do with formal structures more so than with attitudes and feelings. True, God requires righteousness and truth in the inward parts. A person is not pleasing in the Lord's sight until purified to the depths of the inner parts. In our turn, we prefer the kind word and the gentle treatment—that is, except for when it serves to mask formal arrangements that are degrading. The threshold of justice demands that treatment be fair, equitable, and in keeping with the law. Still, we go on causing those moments in which the oppressed could care less about how another feels toward them so long as they are not cheated and treated in an unfair manner.

The happiest state, however, is surely when justice penetrates the heart. Then we experience correspondence between what God requires and the disposition exuded by the countenance. God desires no less from the people of his choice. What God requires is for God's people to live by an order where the dignity of persons is preserved, insured, and not trampled. In the ancient time this confronted the notion that one could come to God on the strength of ritual acts without corresponding acts of love, justice, and compassion. This prophetic word is clarification of what truly matters with God, and this is the clue that is seized upon by the prophet of this generation.

Yes, this is the motif that is manifest in the ministry of the Master—even if this is not the word most often quoted. However, one can see reminiscences of Amos in the prophetic words Jesus spoke: He made it clear that the weighty matters of the law are mercy and justice. (See Mt. 9:13.) He strongly condemned outward shows of piety that had nothing to do with the state of the heart (Mt. 6:1–18). The Lord decried those who honored him with their lips, while their hearts were far from him (Mt. 15:8). No good purpose was served when the content of the lips was for the purpose of hiding what was in the heart.

The issues have not disappeared: The posture of piety is what was stressed again and again in the election of the American president in 2000. True, flaws could be found with the administration that was leaving office, but the ones that battled to replace it showed no clearer presence of righteousness. Instead, one can see in them the flaw Amos addressed: The needy were sold for a pair of shoes; the shekel was made great and the ephah small.

Perhaps it is not fair to place plenary blame on one person; but the one who occupies the White House sets a tone for the nation in matters of justice. The truest measure of justice is the way policies affect the living conditions of the least–the needy, those who live on the margins. The church and the government are measured by looking at the plight of the widows and orphans and of the homeless.

We are seeing a day when the gap is widening between the haves and the have nots. A handful possess the wealth, and the masses languish in poverty. Even among those who name the name of Christ, wealth and prosperity are erected as the measure of piety, when all too often this is the measure of crudity and chicanery.

The gap widens as changes continue to appear in the marketplace: Less room is made for the disadvantaged. The advantage is to those with a profession, an education, or the knowledge to go into business. These traits show the value of frugality, thrift–the marks of those raised in the era and by the values of personal responsibility. But those at the bottom of the social rung are told to exhibit these graces while acts of oppression remove the real possibility of doing so. It is like requiring the making of bricks without straw.

The browning of America is the future of the nation. The question is whether a nation that has systematically denied its blessing to its permanent underclass will amend its ways. Africans were brought as chattel; yellow men were used to build the railways; red men were driven from their land. But those south of the border show little if any respect for the border, and the question is who really won the Mexican War. Little if any correlation exists between the wage that is paid and what it costs to live in the economy. So long as labor is supplied at poverty wages, hopes for improvement remain dim–that is, without the prophetic voice. *Shall this be another group we can exploit by keeping wages depressed below the poverty level and health care benefits out of reach? Shall this group be turned against other groups of workers—with whom, if they joined forces, they could be a majority?*

In the wake of the election, where shall we go from here? This is similar to the question raised by King toward the end of his life. He recognized, as did Amos, that the choice was between chaos and community. The options have not changed from the eighth century B.C.E. to the present.

Let justice roll, let justice roll. Seize the image: justice rolling down like water. We have seen this image before. Rolling water: it is living, pure, refreshing. Indeed, in the rolling it purifies itself of the debris or other dangerous bodies that can lurk within it. Rolling water: this stands in stark contrast to drought.

Righteousness as an ever-flowing stream: This is life and virtue coming down from God for the blessing of the nation. God's way is *the* way: It is not separable from the right relationships ordered from on high. Here there is flow, a surge that is sufficiently powerful to move in a mighty sweep what is not allowed under divine approbation.

There is a river, the streams whereof make glad the city of God—the habitation of the Most High. This is a divine flow, a flow that comes from the throne of God. The power in this flow causes fruit to grow. The stream that flows is *mishpat* (justice); in its path hopes are restored, and the land is healed.

CHAPTER 6

Amos 7:10–17

Exegesis

This passage, a dramatic dialogue between the priest Amaziah and the prophet Amos, not only gives us preachers material for sermons, but it also helps us understand what it means to preach at all. Both of the characters in the dialogue have been set apart for service to God's people. As the dialogue unfolds, the reader can see that Amaziah, in desiring to serve God, actually attempts to block God's message through Amos. Unfortunately for those of us who are ordained, Amos, the layperson, speaks the true word from God. Let us who preach attend to this dialogue, for it has both warning and instruction to us.

Amaziah was the priest at the royal sanctuary at Bethel, founded by Jeroboam I (1 Kings 12:26–33). The establishment of this sanctuary, and the one at Dan, represented the attempt of the Northern Kingdom of Israel to distance itself from the temple in Jerusalem. From its very beginning, therefore, the sanctuary had a political purpose along with its intended religious function.[1] Amaziah's lines in the dialogue indicate that he interpreted his role as protecting the political status quo. He refers to Bethel as "the king's sanctuary," and the "temple of the kingdom" (7:13).

Because Amaziah interprets his position in this way, he considers Amos a threat to political and social stability. Once again, Amaziah's words betray his thinking. He assigns Amos's oracles only to Amos himself, with no consideration that the voice of YHWH might be behind them (v. 11). In defending the religious, political, and social status quo, Amaziah seems to have cut himself off from a genuine word from YHWH. As Virgil Howard points out in his sermon below, Amaziah does not seek to refute Amos's predictions by drawing upon some other theological authority. Instead, he tells Amos to leave, to go back from where he came.

If Amaziah represents established religion, the political control of religion, and the protection of the status quo, Amos represents the freedom of God, the critique by God on the institutions that seek to serve God, and the in-breaking of God's power into institutional rigidity. God is free to call a layperson to proclaim the word that established religious leaders ignore. Amos's words of judgment revealed the corruption of Israelite society, which seemed to be prospering. The opinion of the king, the priest, and the people about Israel was not YHWH's opinion.

The conflict between Amos and Amaziah has numerous contemporary parallels. Indeed, the tension between institutional-ization of religion and prophetic critique is a continual issue for people of faith. Institutions carry on the tradition, but prophetic critique brings the fresh word of God to institutions that become stale or even oppressive.

In reading Amos 7, one cannot help but think of Martin Luther King Jr.'s "Letter from Birmingham City Jail." The clergy of Birmingham wanted to protect the stability of the community and saw the civil rights movement as a threat to that stability. The clergy in Birmingham referred to King as an "outsider," someone who was not where he was supposed to be, much as Amaziah told Amos to go back to the Southern Kingdom of Judah. The judgment of history has demonstrated that King brought the liberating word of God to America and deserves the label of a modern-day prophet.[2]

In the early years of the twenty-first century, the tension between institutions and prophetic critique continues. Pacifists and just-war theorists speak out against war tactics and find that their patriotism is questioned. Those who champion the civil rights of gays and lesbians are derided as a threat to the family. What some consider a threat (as Amaziah considered Amos) may be an eruption of God's power for change.

This passage has much to teach us about our ministry of preaching. Ironically, we preachers stand in the shoes of Amaziah, not Amos, at least as far as our office is concerned. We are the official leaders of the church, called to a role within the institution. The first lesson we ought to learn from this passage is that our true loyalty in our proclamation is to God (the free and often discomforting God), not the institution of the church. We can become so wrapped up in membership figures, finances, and other institutional concerns that we neglect or ignore the call of God to preach the word of judgment that might upset the status quo. We are, indeed, called to care for the institutional needs of the church, but that is not our first loyalty. The pressures to concentrate on the needs of the institution are great but must be resisted as we answer God's call to preach the prophetic word.

Despite this call to listen for God's word over the institutional word, and even though the Old Testament prophets were forerunners of contemporary Christian preachers, we are not all called to be prophets. Sometimes the prophets in our society are laypersons—poets, journalists, writers—who point out injustice, who shine God's light into society's dark corners. Some ordained clergy who have a national audience can fill the role of Amos. Often, such figures are more eloquent than we are and have more time to investigate social issues than we do. In those cases, our task as parish clergy is to support their ministry by preparing our congregations to hear the call to justice and the critique of the status quo.

SERMON

"Priest or Prophet?"

The two characters in this passage are our spiritual ancestors. Amaziah was the priest at the royal sanctuary at Bethel. He was the professional clergy with the proper credentials, the official seal of approval. Amos was the uncertified lay speaker, the prophet who claimed not to be a prophet, the businessman God called to say what the professional clergy dared not say. Amaziah is our spiritual ancestor as one set apart for service to the Lord. Amos is our spiritual ancestor as one who spoke on behalf of God.

Our spiritual ancestors are having a family quarrel. Each one thinks he is doing what God wants him to do. Amos is preaching the hard word of God's judgment. The law courts are corrupt; the poor are neglected; worship does not lead to justice. Amos says he is proclaiming these words because God has called him to proclaim them.

Amaziah thinks his job is to defend the king's sanctuary, to bring a note of common sense to counterbalance the outrageous words of Amos. Amos has just said that the sanctuaries of Israel shall be laid waste and that King Jeroboam II will be killed by the sword. Amaziah doesn't want such hurtful and brash words to go unchallenged on his turf. So, our two spiritual ancestors are on opposite sides and seem to be pushing us to make a choice between them.

We have the benefit of 20/20 hindsight to know that Amos is the hero of this story and the book. We know that even though Jeroboam II was not killed by the sword, Israel was destroyed by the Assyrians, never again to exist in the form it enjoyed during Jeroboam's heyday. The events of history vindicated Amos. So, if the text forces us to choose between Amos and Amaziah, our first impulse is to choose Amos.

Besides the judgment of history, don't we as preachers fantasize about being Amos the prophet or Huldah the prophetess? The prophets bravely proclaim the word and let the chips fall where they may. They have the great sound bites: "Let justice roll down like waters, / and righteousness like an ever-flowing stream." If nothing else, we want to preach with the power and poetry of Amos.

The world needs Amoses. It's almost scary how similar we are in some ways to the Northern Kingdom of Israel in the time of Jeroboam II. Jeroboam opened trade routes and ushered in a time of prosperity. People could build their dream homes of hewn stone with imported Phoenician ivory.

Here and now, the Dow Jones is above 10,000, and the NASDAQ is in record territory [true at the time this was preached]. The U.S. has more billionaires than ever before.

But the downsides are eerily similar, too. Amos blasts the law courts. He lifts up the rug and shows everyone the poor who have been swept under it. He reminds people who don't want to hear it that not everyone has benefited from the new prosperity under Jeroboam.

Today, in spite of the booming economy, the homeless problem is actually worse then it was in the 1980s when everyone was talking about it. One out of four children in Texas lives in poverty. And the law courts? Three times recently, the Texas Court of Criminal Appeals has upheld death sentences when the defendant's lawyer fell asleep during the trial. Some defendants are in jail almost three months before they see a lawyer. We need Amoses.

If Amos is the hero, does that make Amaziah the bad guy? Sermons from the text often portray him as the brown nose who sold out. Instead of caring about the poor, he wanted to keep the king happy. Amaziah apparently didn't draw upon the tradition of Nathan, the courageous prophet who confronted King David with his sins. Amaziah's words to Amos about not preaching such things in the king's sanctuary make him sound like the kind of priest who sucked up to the king and made sure that no important feathers were ever ruffled.

The modern-day Amaziahs don't come off looking too well, either. Modern-day Amaziahs are still trying to shush the prophets. In this postmodern era we consistently see two men as modern-day prophets—Martin Luther King Jr. and Oscar Romero. Both of them encountered people who told them to stop saying what they were saying. Whenever King went out of Alabama, he was told to go back where he belonged, much as Amaziah tells Amos to go back to Judah. In one of his sermons, Romero compared his detractors to modern-day Amaziahs. If we have to choose between Amos and Amaziah, Amaziah is not looking so good. We may be tempted to get a chain saw and cut Amaziah out of our spiritual family tree.

Before we get too carried away in trashing Amaziah, however, we have to remember that he is still our spiritual ancestor. He was a priest charged with care of a flock. We don't like others messing with our flocks. You know how it goes. One of your members has a friend who attends another church. The member goes to a Bible study with her friend. The Bible study is on Revelation. Next thing you know you're having to clean up the mess: raptures, tribulations, mark of the beast, and so forth. Amaziah may have thought he would have to clean up Amos's mess. If anyone needed to preach the hard word to the king, Amaziah would do it himself. If we can't affirm Amaziah, we may at least be able to empathize with him.

It is good that we can empathize with Amaziah. Why? Because, if we are forced to choose between them, we are called more to Amaziah's office than to Amos's. To say that we are called to the office of Amaziah is not to say that we shut our ears to the words of the prophets or that we try to shoo them away. It is not to say that we are called to pamper the rich and powerful in our congregations. We are, nevertheless, called to the long-term care of our flocks, not to short preaching episodes, after which we go back from where we came.

It is not as glamorous or as exciting to be Amaziah as it is to be Amos. We Amaziahs have to get the apportionments in and help find a Sunday school teacher for the middle school. Nevertheless, even though our work is not as glamorous, the church would not survive without us Amaziahs.

If we are the Amaziahs more than we are the Amoses, we do not ignore the word of Amos. Our ministry depends on the ministry of Amos. Ironically, Amaziah himself inadvertently suggested a way to understand our ministries. Amaziah tells the king that the land cannot bear all of Amos's words.

The land cannot bear them. Amaziah makes it sound as though the words coming through Amos from God are weight that the land is not strong enough to carry, almost as though an athlete tried to pick up a barbell that was too heavy. The land cannot bear all of Amos's words.

There are still words out there too heavy for the church to bear. The words about our law courts and about how we treat the mentally ill in this state and throughout the country are sometimes too heavy for the church to pick up. These words may come from preachers in certain pulpits who have the gifts of Amos, from Martin Luther King Jr. and Oscar Romero. They may come from laity, as Amos was. They may come from Toni

Morrison, or Tracy Chapman, or Molly Ivins. If we do not have the gift of Amos for words, our ministry still depends on those words coming to the church, even if they are too heavy for the church to pick up.

If the church is not strong enough to bear those words, maybe that is our ministry. Maybe we are the personal trainers for a spiritually flabby church. The church is too out of shape to pick up the words of the prophets. We who are called to the ministry of Amaziah are to lead the church in spiritual exercise class so that it can bear more and more of that weight.

Sermon

"Showdown at Bethel"

Virgil P. Howard

Anybody with an ounce of common sense could have predicted it—it had to happen. You just can't go around saying things like Amos was saying and not expect sooner or later to end up in serious trouble with some very powerful people. And sure enough, here we are in imagination witnessing the inevitable confrontation between the harsh-sounding, no-holds-barred, tell-it-like-it-is southern preacher—Amos—and the smooth-talking, sophisticated, boss-people-around northern cleric, the representative of power (real power, governmental, social, religious power), Amaziah.

Those who put together the sayings of Amos didn't give us many stories about the prophet, just his words. But here was a story that just *had* to be told. Can't you just see them, standing there in our text, eyeball to eyeball, polite small talk done with, bottom-line confrontation. While our initial reaction might well be to identify with the good guy, Amos, we might just learn more for ourselves and about ourselves if we hold our applause for a few minutes and hear Amaziah out. There may be more to him, and more of him in us, than we would like to think. Amaziah: man caught between king and prophet—man who tries to escape the prophetic word—man who loses everything. And so…Amaziah…we're listening…

One of the first things that strikes us about Amaziah is that he seems to be a person being pulled in two directions. It makes us wonder if he is as convinced about what he is saying as he would like us to believe. On the one hand, he is clearly a loyal civil servant, appointed by the king, in this case a man named Jeroboam, to preside over affairs at the royal sanctuary at Bethel. And so he is responsible not just for any shrine or altar, but for the king's own sanctuary—the symbol of the divine right and status of the king. Beth-el, the house of God, is not just a place of worship. It is also the symbol of peace and unity and stability. And so Amaziah is bound by his loyalty to the one who appointed him.

By the time you and I get in on the confrontation, he has already had a conversation with Jeroboam about the situation. Amos, he has reported, has come from the South and is apparently heading up a conspiracy to overthrow the king and maybe even have him assassinated. He is saying things such asm, "the sanctuaries of Israel shall be laid waste, / and I will rise against the house of Jeroboam with the sword" (7:9). Or: "Jerohoam shall die by the sword, / and Israel must go into exile / away from his land" (7:11). That sounds fairly ominous, and Amos is filling the land with this kind of radical talk. Maybe Amaziah's memory is good, and he reminds the king of other prophets in other times who have meddled in affairs of state. He might have been remembering Elijah and Elisha—Yahweh prophets instrumental in the intrigues that brought Jeroboam's family to power in the first place a hundred years earlier (1 Kings 19:15–18; 2 Kings 9). So Amaziah is not just being paranoid about prophetic speeches—a lot is at stake here: National security is being threatened. Amaziah has been a faithful functionary and warned his king about the threat.

But things are not that simple, for he has also heard something else, another kind of talk from Amos, a kind of talk that has apparently convinced him that Amos is a sure enough prophet of Yahweh. You notice that he doesn't accuse Amos of not being a prophet, or of being a *false* prophet. He uses a particular word when he speaks to Amos: "O seer," he says, *seer,* one of several words used in the Hebrew Bible to designate a prophet, one who speaks God's word for the people. "O seer," he says, "flee away to the land of Judah." "Flee"–it sounds like a warning, doesn't it? "Save yourself! Run for it!" "[E]arn your bread there, and prophesy there." *Just not here at the very heart of royal power and prestige.* We wonder, "What have you heard, Amaziah? What has made you think that Amos might just be for real? That he might be a spokesperson for the God called Yahweh?"

Have you heard Amos say that Israel has behaved shamefully? That while its neighbors on all sides act shamefully by making war against other nations, the wealthy and powerful in Israel have shamed themselves by choosing to make war on their own poor people?! Have you heard that Yahweh *sees* when people make war on poor people and that it grieves God's heart and fires God's anger when poor people are crushed (1:2–2:11)? Is that what you have heard, Amaziah? And do you think there might be something in it?

Or did you hear Amos rant and rave about a society that values the bottom line more than it cares about people at the bottom? A society in which profit is more important than people, and a new pair of sneakers is more valuable than the people that go blind producing them (2:6; 5:11; 8:5)?

Did you perhaps hear Amos warn about the perils of keeping poor people pushed down (2:7; 3:9; 5:11; 6:4–6) and assuming that they will always be satisfied with the crumbs that trickle down from the tables of the rich? Is that what you heard, Amaziah?

Or maybe you heard Amos chastising a society in which rich people, including people in government, can pay for and indulge in all kinds of sexual antics while they criticize the poor for having too many kids (2:7) and refuse to do anything to protect the health of those kids? Or a society in which rich people have several homes (3:15) or luxurious homes (5:11) while the poor sleep in streets and slums?

Or did you hear Amos wonder why the tax structures always seem to favor the haves and punish the have-nots (2:8; 5:11)?

Or did you hear Amos thunder against a legal system in which justice is routinely treated like a commodity the wealthy can purchase while the "little people" go to jail or pay fines or end up in prison, maybe even on death-row (5:7, 12; 8:5)?

Or maybe what really got under your skin, Amaziah, was Amos's accusation against all of the religious activity that folks like you organize and promote—solemn assemblies with singing and sacrificing and praying. Did you hear Amos's claim that all of these religious activities are empty and meaningless and maybe even offensive to God unless justice for God's poor people runs through the streets of your city like a spring flood? Is that what caught your attention, Amaziah? Is that when you not only heard Amos speaking to you, but also when you caught in his words the sound of God's own voice, God's own cry for justice?

Amaziah heard something that caused him to regard Amos as a prophet. But to put all these questions to Amaziah is to ask them of ourselves as well, isn't it? Because what we are finally interested in is not just what Amaziah heard in the message of Amos 2800 years ago, but what we ourselves hear in the words of Amos. I would guess that anyone reading this text from Amos today and reading this sermon on that text knows something of what it feels like to be pulled in different directions. You can identify with Amaziah as he is pulled toward loyalty to the *status quo*. Yes, he is pulled to the way things are. He is pulled to all of the political and social and, yes, religious institutions we create to maintain things as they are. He is pulled toward loyalty toward all of those things that guarantee that we will continue to enjoy the good things of life, our own security and comfort and happiness and privilege. But we also identify with Amaziah as he is pulled in the other direction. Now and then, we know what it means to be pulled into the painful awareness that things can be maintained as they are only at a terrible price, namely our society's own continuing assault on the poor. There seem to be plenty of successors to Amos who remind us of this. Could it be, for example, that Amos comes to us in the pages of the annual United Nations Human Development Report? Recent reports point to some rather gloomy statistics:

FACT: As the twenty-first century began, the world's 225 richest individuals, of whom 60 are Americans with total assets of $311 billion, have a combined wealth of over $1 trillion—equal to the annual income of the poorest 47 percent of the entire world population.

FACT: The richest fifth of the world's people consumes 86 percent of all goods and services, while the poorest fifth consumes just 1.3 percent. Indeed, the richest fifth consumes 45 percent of all meat and fish, 58 percent of all energy used and 84 percent of all paper. This richest fifth has 74 percent of all telephone lines and owns 87 percent of all vehicles.

FACT: At the end of 2002 nearly 42 million people around the world were living with HIV/AIDS. The disease is especially rampant in developing countries and has already killed the mother or both parents of 13 million children.

And on and on and on...

Amaziah, you heard something—was it the cry of God for justice for the poor? Did you feel torn between that cry and loyalty to government and temple that would assure that things stayed pretty much as they were?

We may well recognize ourselves in Amaziah, the man pulled in different directions. Like him, we know that that is not a good way to feel. It's too stressful to be in that predicament for very long. So now we watch Amaziah make his move to get himself out of the bind and save everyone—the king, himself, and even Amos—from a potentially disastrous confrontation. How? The obvious way: Eliminate one of the sources of tension; get rid of one of the things that are tugging at you. In this case: *Send the prophet away.* Create some distance between yourself and that disturbing, threatening prophetic word. Get it at arm's length, at a safe distance. "O seer, go, flee away to the land of Judah." Look, it's only a few miles down the road to the border. Go back home, and do your prophet thing there, anywhere, "but never again prophesy at Bethel, for it is the king's sanctuary, and it is a temple of the kingdom." In other words, do not do it here at the symbolic heart of power. Don't get up in the face of power and challenge its major supporting institutions—especially this house of God!

That seems to be a favorite thing to say to prophets. Centuries later a group of Pharisees would come to Jesus and warn him: "Get away from here, for Herod wants to kill you"

(Luke 13:31). Go somewhere else to talk about your reign of God and how good it is for the poor and powerless.

Again, it would be easy to fall into a condemnation of Priest Amaziah, except that we know how difficult it is to avoid doing a similar kind of thing—how difficult it is to look at the church we love and to which we give a great deal of our time and money and to ask the hard question: To what extent does the church serve as institutional support for governmental and economic structures and policies that are indifferent at best and hostile at worst to the poor and powerless among us? What are the implications of the fact that churches build beautiful new buildings and run wonderful programs and pay folks on staff decent salaries? Is the implication that the church's economic abilities are directly tied to an economic system that leaves millions of people in poverty, unable to take advantage of health care and educational resources?

How easy is it, really, to distinguish in our church life between acts of patriotism and acts of discipleship? What does it mean that a worshiping congregation on Sunday morning mirrors so perfectly the social and economic realities of the society around it? What does it mean that many churches display national flags and sing patriotic songs? Why is it that our own government can so automatically count on church folk to support military actions to punish world leaders who threaten our self-proclaimed interest, even if that involves inflicting untold harm on powerless persons living in that country—for example, in Iraq?

These and many questions like them are not easy to answer. In none of these cases are the issues totally clear and unambiguous. Sometimes conflict rests on valid values. Seldom are we presented with the options right or wrong, good or evil. Frequently Amaziah's solution is *very* tempting, so we find some way to push the painful prophetic challenge away. How do we push it away?

By simply denying that any such problems exist.

Or by blaming the victims—*if they would just work harder*.

Or by being overwhelmed—*the problems are too big for the church to take on*.

Or by defaulting to someone else—*we can't solve the problems of the nation or the world. Our resources are only a drop in the bucket; these are problems of the government and not the church.*

Or by injecting theological nuances into the conflict—*we must guard the boundary between church and state (unless we see federal funds for our programs). Christians ought not to get involved in partisan politics.*

Or by discrediting the prophets who urge us to face these questions—*if the prophet has a sexual affair, for example, then his or her message can be disregarded.*

"Flee, O prophet! Go away! Do your prophesying somewhere else, just not here among us, at our church door!"

And the distancing strategy may work—for a while. But the experience of Amaziah raised another possibility. Amos tells Amaziah: *Because you say "Go away" and "Don't prophesy against us," this is what God says to you:*

> "Your wife shall become a prostitute in the city,
> and your sons and your daughters shall fall by the sword,
> and your land shall be parceled out by line;
> you yourself shall die in an unclean land,
> and Israel shall surely go into exile away from its land."
> (7:17)

These are terrible words, beyond imagination for most of us. But that's what "seers" do, isn't it—see what the rest of us can't see? Prophets are folks who think what the rest of us cannot or will not permit ourselves to think or imagine: *We could lose everything! Everything that we hold so precious—family, country, way of life, life itself.*

So Amos seems to say to Amaziah and to us: To send the prophet away, to ignore the cry for justice that the prophet announces, is dangerous. It is dangerous not only because it condemns the victims of injustice to remain victims, but also because it destroys the lives of those who refuse the prophetic summons. There is, then, a good bit of enlightened self-interest involved in paying attention to this kind of prophetic warning. As one contemporary theologian, Joerg Rieger, is saying: It is time that we Christians in North America get beyond thinking of justice in terms of certain "special interest" groups, and begin thinking in terms of our "*common* interests" in justice issues.³ How long can we live with rampant consumerism, with violence as entertainment, with poverty as acceptable, with profit as ethical norm? And how long can we as Christians stay spiritually alive without facing and dealing with our complicity in the war against the poor? Maybe Amos can help us hear in very concrete terms what Jesus asks the church: "For what will it profit [you] to gain the whole world and forfeit [your] life?" (Mk. 8:36).

So the encounter between Amaziah, priest of power, and Amos, prophet of God, ends with this awful image of disaster. Such an image always comes to those who want to chase away the word of the prophet, who want to ignore the word and sacrifice everything to keep things the way they are. Only tragedy? Or also a word of hope, of gospel?

Amaziah—a person caught between kingly establishment and prophetic challenge, one who pushes the prophetic warning away, one who loses everything—is also a messenger of grace. Thank God for your story. Thank God for those who retold your story again and again as a way of calling faithful people into the conversation with Amos and through him with God. Thank God for continuing to call to people like Amaziah and like us. Yes, thank the God who does not give up on us. Thank God who pursues us and woos us into God's own struggle against mindless allegiance to our own well-being and equally mindless indifference to the poor of the world. Thank God for calling the world of justice and peace into being and moving us closer to the day when all peoples

> shall all sit under their own vines and under their
> own fig trees.
> and no one shall make them afraid;
> for the mouth of the LORD of hosts has spoken.
> (Mic. 4:4)

CHAPTER 7

Introduction to Micah

Micah prophesied at or near the end of the chaotic eighth century B.C.E. By 722, the Assyrian Empire had already defeated the Northern Kingdom of Israel. Almost constant warfare marked the rule of the Assyrian king Sargon II. In 701 his son Sennacherib besieged Jerusalem. Sennacherib's campaign may have been the historic background of military threat as YHWH's judgment on the people of Judah.

Judging from the oracles he left behind, one assumes that Micah was a fiery preacher who defended the cause of the poor, often in forceful and graphic language. In 3:8 Micah described his special commission to declare YHWH's judgment on the "heads of Jacob" (3:1) and on the bought-and-paid-for prophets who refused to confront them (3:5). In opposition to these leaders and prophets, Micah was "filled with power, / with the spirit of the LORD, / and with justice and might" (3:8). He accused the Judean leadership of greed, corruption, and exploitation. The leaders of Judah had failed to protect the vulnerable—widows, orphans, the poor, and small farmers—and so would suffer YHWH's punishment. YHWH's judgment would include the destruction of Jerusalem, a prediction for which Micah was remembered after it came to pass over a century later (3:12).[1]

The delineation of the sections of Micah is disputed. I have chosen to mark off three sections: chapters 1–3, 4–5, and 6–7.[2] Chapters 1–3 contain primarily oracles of judgment denouncing especially the sins of Judah and occasionally the sins of Israel. The passage contained in 2:12–13 is a brief oracle of salvation in which YHWH, speaking in first person, promises to gather the survivors into a new community. The oracle is post-exilic in origin and was inserted by the editor of the book. It brings a welcome word of grace in the midst of the oracles of judgment. Chapters 4–5 contain several oracles that promise that YHWH will act to rebuild and restore, make for peace, and raise up a new king for war-weary Judah. Chapters 6–7 contain a variety of oracles, including courtroom indictment (6:1-2), ethical instruction (6:8), lamentation (7:1-7), and assurances of grace (7:18-20).

In all likelihood, the prophetic oracles that derive from Micah himself are contained in chapters 1–3.[3] Micah's ministry consisted of blistering denunciations of the rich, and passionate defenses of the poor. Centuries later, chapters 4–7, the words of grace and restoration mixed in with lamentation and judgment, were added to give hope to the spiritually depleted exiles. Many commentators have drawn comparisons between Micah and Isaiah, both in form and content.[4] Micah 1–3 compares with Isaiah 1–12 because both contain primarily oracles of judgment, with occasional words of grace. (See Micah 2:12-13 and Isaiah 9 and 11.) Micah 4–5 contains oracles of salvation, which correspond to Isaiah 40–55. Micah 6–7 bears some similarity to Isaiah 56–66, with lamentation, judgment, and oracles of salvation interspersed. As were both Hosea and Amos, Micah is a composite book, written over the course of several centuries. The final product is a rich tapestry of oracles revealing the depth and breadth of the people's relationship with their God.

Because chapters 4–6 are covered in the exegetical treatments below, this section will concentrate on chapters 1–3 and chapter 7.

Chapters 1–3

The opening oracle (1:2-7) in Micah is a dramatic picture of an angry YHWH coming down from heaven in judgment. The prophet reminded his audience that up to that point, YHWH had indulged the sins of humanity. But now, he announced, God was compelled to act. YHWH must leave the holy temple (v. 2b) and walk on earth. The image the oracle presents is of a giant striding over the face of the earth and crushing manifestations of idol worship beneath an enormous heel (v. 3). The imagery becomes more surreal as mountains melt and valleys burst open. These examples of YHWH's wrath sound as if they were drawn from natural phenomena, such as volcanoes (v. 4a), earthquakes (v. 4b), and floods (v. 4c). These forces of nature are concentrated and intensified in Micah's description of YHWH's arrival. As did Amos and Hosea before him, Micah wanted to startle complacent people who underestimated the reality and severity of YHWH's judgment. This oracle speaks of God's power and reminds us how seriously God takes injustice and exploitation.

The book of Amos opened with a description of YHWH's "roar" that dried up the top of a mountain and withered pasturelands (Amos 1:2). Micah portrays YHWH's anger with even more dramatic consequences for nature. The scriptures indicate that humanity is intended to live in harmony with nature, exercising care and responsibility for God's other creatures and the resources of the earth (see Gen. 1:26–28; Ps. 8:5–8). Micah says that the people's sin affects the world of nature; judgment spills over into the rest of God's creation. Contemporary preachers can learn from the prophets' understanding of the interrelatedness of life. Our ecological sins affect nature; they despoil God's creation.

Chapters 2–3 detail the people's specific sins and define the ministry of the historical prophet Micah. In these chapters, Micah both vigorously defends the poor and sternly chastises the rich and powerful. Underlying this section of the book is the conviction that the people of Judah should have worked at building community, with the powerful and secure taking care of the poor and vulnerable. The leaders are the ones who should have understood and promoted justice (3:1–2). The leaders of the community had ignored that obligation, taking every opportunity to enrich themselves (2:2, 9).

Wealthy landowners devised ways, with the aid of corrupt judges, to acquire the fields and houses of those less powerful. Micah became the spokesperson for those who had been cheated out of what was rightly theirs. Micah indicts the prophets of the time for failing in their responsibility. The goal of their preaching was economic security, rather than fidelity to the demands of justice and fairness.⁵ In contrast to them, Micah's ministry was "filled with power, / with the spirit of the Lord, / and with justice and might" (3:8). This verse is as much as we get of Micah's call to preach, but it helps us understand how he understood his ministry. The four terms Micah uses to characterize his ministry connote courage, conviction, strength, energy, and dependence on God. The words for "power" and "might" in this verse were even used for sheer physical strength such as Samson or Gideon might embody (see Judg. 16:5–30 and 8:21). Micah's fortitude in working on behalf of the oppressed can serve as an inspiration to modern-day prophets and prophetesses.

Micah is unrelenting in his attack on the leaders of Judah. He accuses them of lying awake at night plotting evil (2:1) and exploiting the most vulnerable members of society: the poor, women, and children (2:9). Micah's condemnation of the wicked leaders erupts into one of the most shocking metaphors in the Bible. In vivid language, Micah describes the acts of tearing the skin off the people, ripping away their flesh, and chopping up their bones as if to make stew. Micah compares the leaders of Judah to cannibals! While such an image is startling in its impact, it is a compelling reminder of just how much damage is caused to people by impersonal economic systems and political policies.

Despite its revolting image, this section of Micah is valuable for contemporary preaching in several ways. The emphasis in this section on the plight of the poor and on their victimization at the hands of the rich is a topic that cries out for proclamation. Micah identified with those who had lost their inheritance and possessions as "my people" (3:3), a challenge to contemporary preachers to notice who the victims are in their communities and to seek to give voice to their grievances.

Preachers today have an obligation to shine the spotlight on inhuman working conditions, commercialization of children's sexuality, the persistence of slavery in some countries, and other ways in which God's children are "chewed up and spit out" by those callous enough to get rich at the expense of others.⁶

Contemporary preachers can see in Micah's statements about himself in 3:8 a call to courage and integrity. We must be careful to avoid self-righteousness and to be open to critique by others; but we must always remember we are called to proclaim our message with power, justice, and might, and in the Holy Spirit. If we feel compelled to preach a message of judgment or confrontation of evil, Micah 3:8 can help us to reflect on and prepare for that call.

Chapter 7

Because it follows the spectacular promises of chapter 4, the Advent text in chapter 5, and the famous summary of prophetic ethics in chapter 6, chapter 7 may often be overlooked. Although this chapter may not stand out as brilliantly as the other parts of the book, it has an important contribution to make to Micah as a whole, and to contemporary preaching. The chapter consists of two oracles, verses 1–17 and 18–20.

The oracle in 1–17 is a poignant passage that begins in lamentation but ends in triumphant confidence in God's power and reliability. The oracle bears some similarity to the lament psalms, such as Psalms 13 and 22, which begin in distress but end in hope and trust. The tone of the passage is very different from the angry pronouncements in chapters 1–3 and so adds to the emotional depth of the whole book.

As the oracle in 1–17 begins, the prophet, speaking on behalf of the city, is in despair over the people's lack of faithfulness. "Woe is me!" he cries and then develops a simile of a hungry person searching for food. He is starved for faithfulness and compares himself to one who cannot find even a cluster of grapes after both the harvest and the gleaning has picked the vine clean. The description of the evil in the land is a dark, foreboding picture.

No upright people are left; the people act as predators; their only skill is doing evil. The prophet depicts a total breakdown in social relationships. The leaders and judges are greedy and corrupt; friendships cannot be trusted; people in romantic relationships cannot confide in one another; families are dysfunctional. The lack of faithfulness has poisoned every part of life.

Verse 7 serves as a transition between the lamentation and the expression of confidence in YHWH. If the prophet cannot find faithfulness in the people, he can find it in God. Despite the thorough corruption of every aspect of society presented in verses 1–6, the prophet (probably still speaking on behalf of the city) can have confidence in God. The situation itself presents no reason for hope; only in God does the prophet find hope. The prophet's willingness to hope in spite of circumstances is reminiscent of Habakkuk 3:17–19, where even a poor harvest and economic hardship will not prevent the prophet from trusting in God.

The expression of confidence in God in 8–17 acknowledges that the people deserve chastisement for their sins (v. 9), but still trusts that God will restore the people to favor and vindicate them against their enemies, who have taunted them. Even though the oracle is somewhat nationalistic and vindictive, it announces that all people will acknowledge God's power and sovereignty and that even unfaithful Israel will be vindicated.

This oracle has significant preaching value. The central message of the oracle is that our faith is based on God's reliability, not human faithfulness. Every pastor deals with situations in which a prominent leader has disappointed people through some moral lapse. Religious leaders have been found guilty of adultery, embezzlement, alcohol abuse, and a host of other sins. In a sermon from this text, a pastor could help the congregation see that, even though they have been hurt and disappointed many times by others' weaknesses—even leaders—God is still faithful. This passage would be particularly appropriate after a community, denominational, or national scandal has shaken the people's confidence in human leadership.

The passage could serve as well for the preacher's own devotional time. While avoiding self-pity and a sense of superiority, pastors can use the passage to reflect on their own disappointments. Many situations arise that test a pastor's trust in the church. A respected church layperson is caught in an affair. People accept offices in the church, but don't perform the duties. Regular churchgoers hold on to their racist and sexist notions and language. Pastors are also disappointed in their own performances and moral shortcomings. This passage serves as a reminder that even if no one else is faithful, God is faithful. Our ministry is based upon and points to God's faithfulness.

The brief passage that closes the book of Micah, 7:18–20, is a refreshing oracle that celebrates God's forgiveness. The first part of verse 18, "Who is a God like you…?" is a word play on the name "Micah," which translates into the rhetorical question "Who is like YHWH?" The answer, of course, is "no one!" Only God delights in showing clemency; only God does not retain anger; only God is compassionate, faithful, and loyal. In these three verses, the prophet offers three memorable images of God's forgiveness.

The Hebrew words translated as "pardoning iniquity" in verse 18 convey "lifting off," as God takes the weight of guilt off our shoulders. Verse 19 declares that God will tread our iniquities under foot and cast our sins into the depths of the sea. These three images–lifting off, treading underfoot,[7] and casting into the sea–drive home the completeness of God's mercy. Our sins are taken away, crushed, and drowned.

Taken by itself, this concluding oracle is a powerful witness to God's thorough and reliable grace. As such it could serve well as the text of a sermon. In light of the rest of the book of Micah, it balances the stinging rebukes of chapters 1–3 and helps us place God's anger in the context of God's grace.

Theological Reflections on Preaching from Micah

Many intriguing metaphors for God emerge from the book of Micah. God is sometimes the giant who strides the Earth in anger (chap. 1), but also the tender God who "delights in showing clemency" (7:18). Micah also presents unforgettable admonitions for ethical behavior (6:8). Space does not permit us to explore fully the rich theology of this book. Nevertheless, two themes that deserve discussion emerge. The first is the tension throughout the book between the vigorous proclamation of God's judgment and the assurances of God's grace and forgiveness. The second is the role of the preacher in addressing issues of poverty.

As did both Hosea and Amos, the book of Micah includes oracles of grace along with pronouncements of judgment. As they did in Hosea, the oracles of grace in Micah erupt unexpectedly in the midst of words of judgment. For example, in Micah 2:12–13 an oracle promising that YHWH will "gather the survivors of Israel" pops up right between a passage condemning the clergy for "uttering empty falsehoods" and one that accuses the leaders of Judah[8] of hating good and loving evil. Although these two verses 12–13 are almost certainly a post-exilic addition, the rhetorical effect of the final form is startling. Psychologically, the words of grace provide a bit of relief from the anger of the denunciations. Theologically, this brief passage reminds us of the surprising nature of grace. God's grace intrudes where we least expect it.

Although the book of Hosea also contains these sudden jumps to grace in the middle of condemnation, Micah's understanding of grace has a different emphasis than Hosea's. Whereas the emphasis in Hosea is on grace as God's vulnerability, the emphasis in Micah is on grace as God's restoration.[9] A clear affirmation of God's grace comes in chapter 4, which describes the establishment of "the mountain of the LORD's house." The chapter contains the assurance that God will end division among people, abolish the alienation between God and people, and ensure the security that would enable people to abandon their means of protection. As a wonderful addendum (which does not appear in the parallel in Isaiah 2), the passage makes a point of including persons with disabling conditions in the time of restoration.

The emphasis on God's grace as restoration helps us to interpret God's judgment. God judges those things that deny or inhibit the kind of community and harmony described in chapter 4. God's wrath is a means toward establishing the kinds of relationships promised in chapter 4. Even God's judgment can be seen as good news to those who are denied justice, because God cares about their plight.

The second item for theological reflection is closely related to the first. Micah was a strident champion for the poor, eloquently denouncing those who exploited them. He was convinced that God judged the rich who took advantage of the poor and that God's judgment would affect the whole nation. Micah felt such an attachment to those who had been deprived of justice that he referred to them as "my people" (2:9). One clear way in which contemporary preachers can emulate the prophet Micah is to speak out on issues of poverty.

Poverty is a complex problem, having both "top-down" and "bottom-up" causes. The "top-down" causes of poverty are such things as tax codes, minimum wage laws, lack of educational opportunities, and lingering racism that can only be addressed by those who hold power. The "bottom-up" aspect of poverty is that despair often leads to drug abuse, crime, teenage pregnancy, school dropout, and other self-defeating behaviors. The poor themselves have some ability to address these issues.

Although Micah's concern seems to have been primarily with the top-down causes of poverty (unfair judicial systems, confiscation of land), the contemporary preacher may have to address both causes of poverty.[10] Perhaps the preacher's social location may affect which side gets the most attention. Micah calls preachers who serve congregations with influential members to address the "top-down" causes of poverty. Preachers who serve congregations in inner city or rural areas may perceive a need to address both causes. Preachers in all situations must shine the light on the political, social, and legislative resources that can alleviate poverty. When preachers are told to "stick to religion and stay out of politics," we have the book of Micah as our mandate to address how political, business, and religious leaders treat the poor.

CHAPTER 8

Micah 4:1–7

Exegesis

The real power of this passage comes not just from its triumphant message, but also from its placement in the book of Micah. The placement of this poem right after the oracles of chapters 1–3 was a stroke of genius on the part of the final editor(s) of Micah. This beautiful statement of God's healing, community-building, restorative grace provides balance for the harsh but necessary words of chapters 1–3.

The elements of the poem itself are inspiring, no matter who wrote it. The temple in Jerusalem will be raised up to become a kind of beacon to attract all humanity. YHWH's sovereignty will thereby be universally recognized. All people will be eager to draw upon YHWH's instruction. YHWH will establish justice, peace, and security. In the well-known words, the nations of the world "shall beat their swords into plow-shares, / and their spears into pruning hooks; / nation shall not lift up sword against nation, / neither shall they learn war any more"(4:3). The poem implies that God will break down barriers of nationality, religion, and anger over past injustices. YHWH will act to establish the sort of trust between people that will enable people to abandon military weapons and strategies.

The placement of the poem right after the oracles of the historical Micah is important, because the poem reminds us not only of God's forgiving grace along with judgment, but also of what only God can do. The oracles in chapters 1–3 represent God's expectations that Israel will work for justice. The poem in chapter 4 represents the recognition that only YHWH can truly establish a lasting and just peace.

The church proclaims this passage in light of the eschatological promises of the New Testament. Micah 4:1–7 uses the evocative, but imprecise, language of poetry. It does not say when or how God will act to fulfill these promises. Will these things occur within history, or eschatologically? Likely, the poem envisions God acting within history to bring all people together and to manifest God's sovereignty. The poem does not seem to envision a new creation or the passing away of this creation.

In light of New Testament eschatology, the church can proclaim this poem as suggestive of what God's lasting reign in a new creation will be like. God's new creation will include peace, justice, true fellowship, and the nearness and authority of God. The work of the church is to bear witness to what God will do and is doing by its work for relative justice and its proclamation of God's intervention to redeem all of creation.

The book of Micah in its final form is good news, despite the thundering of the historical Micah's oracles in chapters 1–3:

1. It confirms God's care for the poor and oppressed.

2. It wraps God's judgment in oracles of grace like chapter 4.

3. It assures us that even if our stumbling efforts to achieve justice fail, God can work through and beyond history to achieve what we cannot.

Our efforts to work for justice and peace can always be only partially successful. Fear, mistrust, and greed are too deeply entrenched in human nature for us to effect the vision of Micah 4:1–7. Nevertheless, God will reveal God's sovereignty, bring us together, and grant us peace.

Sermon

"A Breath of Fresh Air"

I have forgotten what we were arguing about. Annual Confer-ence meetings can sometimes erupt into heated discussions, and the North Carolina Conference was no different when I was a member of it. Whatever the discussion was about, I do remember that our nerves were frayed. The tension had seeped into our shoulders, not to mention our temples. These discussions at Annual Conference are important. Part of our work as the church is to hammer out stands on controversial issues. Though important, such discussions are stressful, and we were certainly stressed out.

Just as everyone's last nerve was about to snap, a group of pastor's wives walked out onto the platform. With the wife of a district superintendent directing them, the women raised their voices in song. No one had expected them; they weren't on the agenda, but they were just what we all needed. Their beautiful harmony melted away the tension, and we all rose in spontaneous applause, refreshed by their singing. With that breath of fresh air filling our spirits, we went back to work.

The first three chapters of Micah represent important work, as well. Micah confronted the corrupt leaders of Israel and Judah, exposing their hypocrisy. They had claimed moral leadership, but they did not know justice. They stole the land of others who were less powerful (2:2); they tossed widows out of their homes (2:9). The religious leaders were greedy, selling their words to the highest bidder (3:5).

Micah understood his call as standing toe to toe with this greed and hypocrisy. It was not easy work, but Micah did it courageously. Micah stretched the bounds of good taste when he accused the leaders of Israel and Judah of symbolic cannibalism: they chewed people up and spat them out. In the first three chapters, Micah prophesied about an angry God, who punished injustice, corruption, and greed. God's footsteps would crush mountains; valleys would melt like wax before a fire (1:3-4). The wretched leaders would beg for mercy (3:4), and Jerusalem would become a heap of ruins (3:12).

That's where things stand at the end of chapter 3. Anger, hostility, and tension fill the air. Micah has done his duty: he has stood up for those who had no one else to stand up for them. It wasn't easy for Micah, and he tells us that he grieves over what he had to say (1:8-9). There is nothing pretty about these first three chapters. They represent the hard grueling work of being a prophet, of doing what God has called you to do.

What God had called Micah to do was to proclaim God's judgment on the leaders' sins. The leaders needed to hear of God's wrath, of God's power, of God's care for widows, orphans, the poor, the defenseless, and the down and out. Micah's call was not an easy one, and his words are not easy to read. Micah's oracles leave us stressed and tense, and maybe even a little apprehensive of this powerful God.

When we move down one more verse to chapter 4, however, suddenly the words break through like a sweet, harmonious song. Instead of the anger and denunciations of chapters 1–3, chapter 4 stirs us with a grand vision of God's grace, mercy, and redeeming love. The whole mood changes in the blink of an eye. Chapters 1–3 thundered; this chapter soars. Maybe the editors of the book knew what the pastors' wives in North Carolina knew. They knew we needed a breath of fresh air. So the editors put in this poem about God's creative grace. We know Micah didn't write the poem himself, because almost the same poem, in a slightly shorter version, appears in the second chapter of Isaiah. Probably, it was a familiar poem, so Isaiah and Micah both used it. Whoever wrote it, it is just what we need at this point in the book.

After hearing Micah's blistering words in the first three chapters, we need to hear this poem's sparkling melody. The poet's words transform the tension and anger of the first three chapters into confidence in God's renewing power. Instead of accusation, we get affirmation. Promise after promise tumbles from the poet's pen. The God whose feet would angrily crush mountains in chapter 1 is now the God who will raise up a mountain to symbolize stability. In biblical thought, a mountain could represent the connection between heaven and earth. So God will raise up this mountain to bridge the gulf between us and God.

It doesn't stop there. Not only will we be more closely connected with God, but we will also be brought together with each other. God will come to us by means of this mountain, but we will come together at the foot of this mountain as well.

Think of it! During Micah's time, the Assyrians were circling like wolves, licking their chops over Israel and Judah. Later the Babylonians dragged Judah's leaders into exile. In the midst of all that hostility, the poet declares that the Assyrians, the Babylonians, and all the rest will be rushing to God's mountains like teenagers to a Britney Spears concert! Can we imagine today the governments of Iraq, China, and North Korea jostling for a place to sit at God's mountain? We will all feed our faith with God's teachings, with no more cynicism or resistance.

Then, in one of the most beautiful images in all of scripture, the poet describes people beating their swords into plowshares and their spears into pruning hooks. Weapons of death will become tools to grow food for life. People will be so eager for peace that they will engage in hard work to transform the means of death into tools for life. Can we even let ourselves believe in a time when all the nukes will be shut off, the stockpiled weapons will be gone, and our fears about whose finger is on the button will have evaporated?

Peace with God and peace with each other would be grace enough, but Micah's version of the poem adds one more promise. Those who are lame, those who are ill, those who have been outcasts will be gathered for a special blessing. No one is forgotten; no one is unnoticed.

It all sounds too good to be true, but maybe that is what God has in store for the creation. At least the poet thought so. In the midst of an angry book, full of fury and pulpit-pounding wrath, this poem is a breath of fresh air. We need this breath of fresh air, because we have our work cut out for us, just as Micah did. God calls us to speak out for the poor, for those treated unfairly, for those who are pushed out of the way in the mad dash for even more money, for those who are chewed up and spit out by the powerful.

Micah spoke out for those who had been driven from their homes (2:9). Today, more and more children and young women are homeless because of the gap in wealth in our country. While the stock market rose to dizzying heights in the 1990s, a subculture of poverty hid behind its shadow. Many in this subculture are small children and their harried mothers.

According to Anna Quindlen, a columnist for Newsweek, "There are hundreds of thousands of little nomads in America, sleeping in the back of cars, on floors in welfare offices or in shelters five to a room."[1] Micah will not permit us to forget them. They need our voices speaking out for them and our hands ministering to them.

Micah spoke out about people being metaphorically eaten alive (3:2–3), as though by cannibals. Today cruel bosses who care only for the bottom line treat people as virtual slaves. According to reports, perhaps as many as one million people, primarily immigrants, are forced to work in the sex industry or as domestic servants or in fields. We have trouble believing such atrocities are possible in the United States. Often these abused people have no way of escaping their situation because they cannot afford attorneys and don't know to whom they can turn. They are frequently tortured and abused.[2] Micah awakens our outrage and calls us to give a voice to those like these modern-day slaves, whose skin is torn off their backs and whose bodies and souls are chopped up like meat for a kettle (3:2–3).

Micah spoke out against judges who took bribes (3:11) and against corruption in the legal system. Today, judges are influenced by campaign contributions.[3] According to one study, serious errors were found in 68 percent of death penalty cases since the 1972 Supreme Court ruling that reinstated the death penalty in this country.[4] Micah calls us to speak out for justice and fairness in our legal system.

In chapters 1–3, Micah shines a light on the dark corners of injustice, the treatment of the poor, greed, and corruption. His ministry inspires our ministry of shining such a light where those dark corners exist. That can be difficult work. Micah 4 reminds us that while we are working, God is working, too. The poet sings of God's mountain, where we will all come together, where we will be reconciled to God and to one another. As we work for justice, as we raise our voices for the poor, the homeless, and the slaves to American greed, let us listen to the poet's song, refreshing us, energizing us, and giving us the spiritual strength to keep going.

Sermon

"A Vision in Stained Glass"

David Schnasa Jacobsen

A church in Pennsylvania from the early part of the twentieth century has a "Peace Window." You know, one of those stained-glass representations of the hope for peace. The window features children looking on adoringly as a blacksmith beats a WWI canon into plowshares. Yet as you look at the window, you can't help but be struck by how the dream has seemed to grow old. Perhaps the dream of peace, like a 1920's stained-glass window, is a fragile thing.

No doubt the prophet Micah would understand. He offers a powerful picture of peace. His vision soars; his dreams reach high. Yet in the end, his vision is also fragile when you consider what it has witnessed over the years: the violence of empires, the carnage of World Wars, and plain old human cruelty.

Make no mistake: the picture is beautiful. Micah envisions all God's peoples living in peace. Weapons have been turned into farm implements. Everybody has enough food and a place to lay one's head down in peace. Sounds nice, doesn't it? A world where violence is but a distant memory and everyone, yes, everyone, has a share in God's fruitful bounty. It's like that poster that showed up a while back: "Some day schools will have all the money they need, and the military can hold a bake sale!" We can imagine a world like that: a world where we transform weapons into tools and where there is food enough at the "welcome table."

Yet part of us is not so sure about such visions. It just feels too fantastic, too utopian. Visioning such peace with justice comes hard in a day like ours, where every social dream seems trumped by the bottom line of global capitalism. After all, military companies still do a brisk business–and as for land redistribution, it probably doesn't appear under any NAFTA protocols or World Bank agenda items. So part of us shrinks from hopeful dreaming. Yet even a vision has its roots in the ground somewhere.

So perhaps Micah can help us see our own world a little more clearly. There is, after all, a tank factory in Strelna near St. Petersburg. Since the end of the cold war, some 3,000 decommissioned tanks have lain idle there: row upon row of long-parked tanks, with guns grown discolored from disuse. Yet now this old factory has been given the green light—not to make more tanks, but to turn eighty of the tanks into scrap metal for use elsewhere. The factory bosses had hoped to keep the news secret. But eventually good news like that gets out.

Micah would understand, for his compelling vision continues to live even in our jaded hearts: a warring world's hope that swords can turn into plowshares. Micah paints a beautiful picture of peace for all.

But look again! Micah's peaceful vision also assumes all nations will *want* to do God's will. Following our own interests just won't do. When Micah's visionary peace happens, nations will *desire* to do God's will. The prophet is quite specific. The vision of peace presupposes all peoples seeking what God wants. How does Micah put it? "Peoples shall stream to it, / … and say, / 'Come, let us go up to the mountain of the LORD, / …that he may teach us his ways'" (4:2).

Micah's vision is quite clear. The way to the universal peace of swords into plowshares, and vines with fig trees for everybody, passes through the mountain of the Lord, Zion, where God's instruction is sought and given. Hard to imagine, isn't it? Can you see the well-heeled, moneyed policy-makers of George Bush's Washington, D.C., trying to decide whether the rich should get tax cuts by discerning what God wills for the poor? Or try to envision heavy-medaled Pentagon brass around a conference table considering the future of Star Wars missile systems and death-dealing smart bombs in light of psalmic wisdom: "Some trust in chariots and some in horses, but we trust in the name of the LORD our God" (Ps. 20:7, NIV). Or imagine the suits in the corporate boardroom of a pharmaceutical company thinking about what God would say about drug marketing ploys that only raise healthcare costs for society's weakest members. Well, strange as it sounds, this is the world Micah envisions: a place where peace is based on God's will, a peaceful world that heeds God's law.

Of course, that's precisely the problem: Our world right now doesn't work that way. Most people don't walk in God's name. The reality is stark—our world doesn't seek God's will. Consider issues of world peace. For us in North America, the way to peace is found through pursuing national self-interest. Oh, sure, we like to talk about multilateralism from time to time. But in reality we view peace more as the product of national will and interest—call it "peace through strength."

As for vines and fig trees, well, they are usually distributed not according to God's law, but the law of supply and demand. We have our gods, all right: the gods of the marketplace. Who needs the tired old God of the Bible, when Adam Smith's "invisible hand" will do, guiding buyers and sellers to the economic nirvana of lower costs and maximized profits? We don't need God's will when we have a national defense and NAFTA to enforce our own will in the world.

No doubt Micah would understand. Despite his soaring visions, he is all too aware of the sad state of affairs of his day. Micah is prophesying at a time of upheaval in Judah. Under pressure from Syria and Samaria to join a coalition against the powerful Assyrians, the king may be forced to play the kind of power politics that would benefit the elites of all the countries involved. Yet Micah points out that Jerusalem's prominence did not and will not emerge through the political intrigues of power elites. Rather, any hope for the people lies in God's hands, the God who will one day make Jerusalem what they can only dream of. Still, we are tempted to manufacture on our own terms and according to our own interests what only God can give as a gift. That is the way of the world: the pursuit of our own interests. Our world prefers our own will to God's.

But here's the good news: Even now God is doing the work of peace. He is gathering broken folks like us into a new people. God will give us peace by piecing together our brokenness. Micah, you see, was no out-of-touch idealist. He gave voice to a vision, yet also saw his world as it really was. So whatever hopes Micah has are pinned ultimately on God: "The lame I will make the remnant," the prophet says on God's behalf, "and those who were cast off, a strong nation" (4:7).

Micah's vision was not the hope for something better for those who already had it good. Micah's vision was hopeful precisely because it met a nation where it was most broken. God, you see, would make the peaceful vision not so much by executive fiat, as by piecing the broken together. Yet we, of all people, should not be surprised. We who are bound together by gracious symbols of a broken body and blood poured out should know. It's just how God operates.

God pieces together a peace by giving broken bread to a broken people. There's a story about Victoria Woosley in Loveland, Ohio. She's helped put together a Y2K quilt called: "Swords into Plowshares." When you look at it, it's hard to tell what you are seeing: are the pictures on the quilt squares sharp blades of war, or instruments of peace? The artist is clear: some of the squares do commemorate victims of inhumanity, yet others celebrate those who stand for peace with justice. So it is with God's vision of peace: it incorporates those who are broken, who've been laid low by violence, whom God pieces together into a new vision of hope.

So how can that little church in Pennsylvania look at their fragile peace window and not turn away disillusioned? Perhaps the fragility of stained-glass visions like Micah's are precisely their beauty. Visions like swords into plowshares are not just utopian dreams, nor are they excuses to pursue our own interests. For those who look closely, who also look *through* the fragility of the stained glass, it is clear. God takes the broken panes, the jagged shards of our humanity, and in grace pieces them together—so we might see clearly again.

CHAPTER 9

Micah 5:1–5a

Exegesis

Micah 5 is of great value to the church because it conveys a significant reality check concerning God's providential care. This passage reminds us that God is not at our beck and call and that sometimes we must live on hope, waiting for God's time to act.

Although this passage does push us to deeper spiritual insight, preachers would likely pass it by if Matthew 2:6 did not quote it. That citation brings the text to light and adds another dimension to its interpretation. This is a valuable pericope on many levels. It speaks a message from its original context and also through its use in the church's christological reflection.

This passage does not yield its insights easily, however. It is loaded with interpretive problems. Researchers cannot agree on the unity of the passage, its historical background, or the translation of verse 1.[1]

The questions of unity and historical background are related. The final form of the passage is obviously a message to the exiles after the Babylonian defeat of Jerusalem. Some characteristics of the passage suggest that some of the sayings come from an earlier time, however. The primary questions about the unity of the passage concern verse 1 and verse 5a. James Mays, for example, suggests that verse 1 comes from the time of the Babylonian siege of Jerusalem, but that verses 2 and 4 come from a time near the end of the eighth century

B.C.E., around the time Micah may have been active. Verse 3 is then a later interpolation.[2]

The other issue is the phrase in verse 5a, "and he shall be the one of peace." Some commentators consider this to be the beginning of the next unit, although it fits in well with the thought of verses 1–4. As they now stand, the four verses constitute a carefully edited unit composed of strands from various places.[3]

A quick look at different translations reveals the baffling array of renderings for verse 1. The different versions suggest three options for understanding the verse. The first option, defended by Mays and Smith, is that verse 1 refers to self-mutilation: cutting oneself either out of grief or as an attempt to curry favor with God (see also the Tanak; HCSB; NET).[4] The second option, following the Septuagint's reading, is that verse 1 refers to a wall around Jerusalem—either a "wall" of enemy soldiers, or that the walls around Jerusalem have become a trap (see NRSV; New Jerusalem; REB, NAB[5]). The third option is that the verse calls the people to marshal their troops to fight off the siege (NIV, NLT, NASB, ESV, *God's Word*, NKJV; TEV[6]).

A clear determination is difficult to make. Any of the three renderings fits the context, and the Hebrew root *gdd,* used twice in this verse, can mean either to cut oneself or to gather troops. It is used in both senses elsewhere in the Old Testament. In 1 Kings 18:28 it describes ritual cutting by Baal worshipers; in 1 Samuel 30:8 it refers to a marauding band. I am most persuaded by the translation to marshal troops, since cutting oneself was not a Hebrew practice, and marshalling troops makes sense in a siege. In any case, the image is one of panic and futility in response to the advancing army.

What is clear is that the final form of the passage addresses a time of desperation. The Babylonian army has crashed through the gates of the city, and chaos reigns. The soldiers have humiliated the people's ruler by striking him on the cheek, a deep insult. The people are defenseless; the ruler is helpless to repel the attack.

Verse 2 shines as a ray of hope in the darkness of verse 1. A new ruler will arise from a place that, on the one hand, is unlikely, but on the other hand has historical precedent. Bethlehem was a small town, an unlikely place to produce a ruler. Nevertheless, Bethlehem was the home of King David, the mighty monarch who united Israel and led it in its glory days.

If the present ruler has been humiliated, the new ruler will be strong, nurturing, and protective (v. 4). Once again, the kingdom of Israel will extend its influence far and wide ("to the ends of the earth"). The ruler will be strongly connected to YHWH ("in the strength of the LORD"). Verses 2 and 4 paint a picture of restored Davidic glory, a messianic ideal for the besieged people of Judah. Such a promise would be comforting, reassuring, and uplifting during the time of the exile.

Verse 3 is the sobering splash of cold water for the readers of this passage, however. Verse 3 declares that "he [YHWH] shall give them up until the time / when she who is in labor has brought forth." This phrase could refer to the birth of an actual baby or it could be a metaphor.[7] Micah promises God's intervention, but cautions that it will come in the future, not now. YHWH will provide a ruler for the people, but not in time to stop the Babylonians. For now YHWH will give the people up, relinquishing them to the power of the enemy crashing through the gates of the city. The time of salvation is not yet.

The issues in this passage go to the heart of what it means to have faith in God. The church must hold on to its faith in a time when many people feel as though they have been "given up." We feel ourselves to be "given up" to illness, grief, financial problems, joblessness, and the fear caused by terrorists. In its context in Micah, the passage speaks to those who ask why God doesn't intervene to prevent suffering and evil. Why have we been "given up"?

Micah does not specifically answer the question of why. The Babylonian exile was often understood as a punishment for Judah's sins. (See Mic. 3:12.) Certainly, though, it is much too simplistic to see all suffering as punishment for sin. The reasons for suffering remain a mystery. As the psalmist says, if we try to understand suffering, our own or others, it is a "wearisome task." (Ps. 73:16). The focus in Micah 5 is on waiting in faith and hope for God to send the new ruler. Faith is difficult to maintain when one feels "given up."

Nevertheless, Micah's words ring with confidence that God will act, that God will intervene, that God will protect and restore. Micah 5 can be preached any time of the year to address those whose faith is faltering while waiting for God's presence and power in a time of suffering. A preacher could draw connections between Micah 5 and Romans 8:18–27, where Paul talks about the creation groaning while it waits for the Eschaton. Our waiting is agonizing, but we wait in hope, sustained by the Holy Spirit.

Micah 5 is also an Advent text. It appears in Year C on the fourth Sunday of Advent and is paired with Luke 1:39–55, split into two pericopes by the lectionary committee, with Mary's Magnificat serving as a Psalter reading. The passage from Luke promises good news to the downtrodden. Mary proclaims that God has "lifted up the lowly; / he has filled the hungry with good things" (Luke 1:52b–53a). Micah 5 and our own experience remind us that Mary's words are only partially fulfilled at best. The poor often feel "given up" to forces more powerful than they. We still wait, both for the fulfillment of Micah's promises of protection and nurture, and for the poor to be filled with good things.

Micah 5 is quoted in Matthew 2:6, a text that appears every year in the lectionary on Epiphany Sunday, and on the first Sun-day of Christmas in year A. A good understanding of Micah 5 can add depth to preaching on Matthew 2. The New Testament writers saw in Micah 5 a way to help interpret the coming of Jesus.

Jesus fulfills the role of the new leader, the one who nourishes and protects (Mic. 5:4). Jesus was not born until five centuries after the final form of Micah 5 was written, another reminder that God acts in God's time, not ours. Micah 5 reinforces one of the themes of Matthew 2. Herod kills all of the male children under two in Bethlehem. The families of those children are "given up" to the evil of Herod's arrogance. God acts graciously and powerfully by sending the ruler, both the ruler referred to in Micah's original prophecy and the ruler present in Bethlehem's Jesus. God's grace, power, and will for peace sustain us in our times of pain and grief.

Sermon

"A Strange Hope"

As most of you know, I usually read the scripture passage on which I preach from the *New Revised Standard Version* of the Bible. This morning I will read from the *New International Version*. Verse 1 of our passage is very difficult to translate, and I agree more with the NIV than I do with the NRSV. It is not even clear that verse one goes with verses 2–5, but I think that it does.

We have three options for understanding the Hebrew for verse 1. The first is that it refers to gashing oneself. The Jewish translation known as the Tanak prefers this reading.[8] Ancient Near Eastern people would sometimes cut themselves as an expression of grief, not a practice I recommend. If that understanding of the verse is correct, then it calls for the people to gash themselves out of grief for what is about to happen to them.

The second option, the one the NRSV chooses, is to render the verse, "You are walled around with a wall."[9] That could mean one of two things. Either the walls around the city are now a trap because of the advancing troops, or the advancing troops are themselves a wall around the city, a wall of soldiers.

The third option, used by NIV,[10] is that the verse is a call to muster the troops because of the advancing armies. In any case, what we do know is that the passage was written in a time of war when the people faced a crisis. Hear now the words of the prophet Micah:

> Marshal your troops, O city of troops,
> for a siege is laid against us.
> They will strike Israel's ruler
> on the cheek with a rod.
>
> "But you, Bethlehem Ephrathah,
> though you are small among the clans of Judah,
> out of you will come for me
> one who will be ruler over Israel,
> whose origins are from of old,
> from ancient times."

> Therefore Israel will be abandoned
> until the time when she who is in labor gives birth
> and the rest of his brothers return
> to join the Israelites.
> He will stand and shepherd his flock
> in the strength of the LORD,
> in the majesty of the name of the LORD his God.
> And they will live securely, for then his greatness
> will reach to the ends of the earth.
> And he will be their peace.

One of the most vivid images from the decade of the 1970s is film footage of a helicopter taking off from the roof of the U.S. embassy in Saigon. The date was April 30, 1975. The war in Vietnam was supposed to be over. North Vietnamese troops were advancing south. Inside the helicopter were the last remaining American diplomats, military advisers, and some South Vietnamese allies who were leaving before the troops arrived.

People still on the roof were desperately grasping at the helicopter trying to get on, but there was no more room. The helicopter took off. Those on board were flown to safety. Those left behind were at the mercy of the advancing troops. As they watched the helicopter shrink into the horizon, they must have wondered, "What will happen to us?"

Micah's congregation was wondering what would happen to them. The troops were advancing on the city. It was time to sound the alarm and prepare for a siege, but they didn't know if they had the military might to defend themselves. The people of Israel and Judah had to do all of this more than once. In 722 B.C.E., the Assyrians captured Samaria and destroyed the Northern Kingdom of Israel. In 701, they attacked Jerusalem, which barely survived. In 586, the Babylonians attacked Jerusalem, and it didn't survive.

The people, who understood themselves to be God's chosen people, had to endure defeat, the taunts of the victorious enemy soldiers, and, as verse 1 says, they had to endure watching their leader humiliated. When the Babylonians captured Judah, they treated King Zedekiah terribly, in the end blinding him. As the people watched the advancing troops, they were desperate for any hope they could find.

Micah tells them their hope will come from a place they do not expect it. Their hope will come from Bethlehem, a small city in Ephrathah. What is even more surprising than the hope's point of origin is how the hope will come. Micah's congregation likely expected that if God were going to act, God would send tall, strong soldiers who would bravely defend the city against the attacking army.

Instead, Micah tells them of a woman in labor who will give birth to a baby. We can almost hear Micah's congregation crying out in protest, "What good is a baby to us now? Even if this baby is the mightiest warrior of all time, it will be twenty years before he can fight. The troops are surrounding the city now. We haven't got time to wait for a baby to grow up!"

Micah knows they are right. Verse 3 of chapter 5 seems to acknowledge that the people will lose. The NIV translates verse 3 as "Israel will be abandoned." The NRSV says, "he shall give them up." Micah seems to be saying that God will not spare the city; God will not protect them. The hope that Micah offers is not that everything will be OK, that at the last minute God will somehow come through and drive the invading army out. The hope that Micah offers is that God will work through, after, and in spite of the military defeat. Micah offers an image of a time after the defeat when a new leader will arise in Israel, a leader who will take care of and defend the people. This new leader will shepherd Israel like a flock. The people's hope is in the birth of this child.

We know that the New Testament writers look to this particular passage to help explain the birth of Jesus. Just as Micah offers hope in the birth of a child, so the New Testament writers tell us that in the birth of Jesus we have hope. The New Testament writers look to Micah, not because he had a crystal ball to predict the birth of Jesus of Nazareth, but because the prophets had insight into the ways of God. God does what we do not expect.

If we expect that the birth of the Savior means that all our problems will clear up and go away, Micah and the New Testament tell us that that is not how God works. The birth of the baby Micah writes of did not stop the advancing troops. The birth of Jesus did not drive out the hated Roman soldiers from Judea. Through the centuries, the birth of Jesus has not prevented wars, illness, poverty, or suffering.

As much as we might want it to, the birth of Jesus does not reach into our lives and fix everything that is wrong. And sometimes a lot can be wrong in our lives. Sometimes, even the holiday season can be as much a burden as a joy. Sometimes, the holidays can remind us of what is wrong in our lives, when the rest of the time we can put it out of our minds. It's almost as if the holidays can shine a spotlight on our problems. Some of us enter the holidays with family problems. Some of us face problems at work. Some of us have health problems. Amidst the Christmas cheer, the pain of life goes on. A year or so ago, We heard on the radio about a little girl with inoperable cancer who was hoping to live until Christmas. Her last wish was for a lot of Christmas cards. Now her family must look back at Christmas as a time of loss and grief.

The birth of the Savior doesn't keep those kinds of things from happening. But remember one of the names that the Messiah carries: "Emmanuel," God *with* us. The birth of the Savior does not protect us from suffering, even at Christmas time. But the birth of the Savior is our assurance that God is with us, even in the deepest of our pain. The birth of Christ is our promise that God is still at work through and beyond the pain of life. When we wonder, "What will happen?" when we see the troubles of life advancing on us like an army, even at Christmas, let us remember that in it all, God is with us.

Sermon

"Micah's Christmas Surprise"

Micah 5:2–5a and Matthew 2:1–6

Page L. D. Creach

Advent 2000

(This sermon is dedicated to Carnegie Presbyterian Church, in small, Carnegie, Pa., for their great hope in Christ at work through the church.)

> But you, O Bethlehem of Ephrathah,
>   who are one of the little clans of Judah,
> from you shall come forth for me
>   one who is to rule in Israel.
>
> (Mic. 5:2)

Prayer

Lord, Give us faith and love in action, that grows above the noise and strife of our lives until we understand that God is here, bringing and expecting justice and peace.

Micah's prophetic words had to surprise many people. And surprises can be great or grim. It depends on the difference between what you are expecting and what you are receiving. For example, I wanted a trampoline for Christmas one year. A friend in Virginia introduced me to all the bouncy, up and down, hopping and spinning, flipping and flopping fun I could have on it.

I jumped all day. I was encouraged to get off of it to have some lunch, but I kept jumping. They came back too soon and said to get off of it because it was time for dinner. I don't really remember; but it seems like I was still jumping when it was time for breakfast, and they were forced to call my parents to come and get me off of it. I loved the trampoline. I really wanted one for Christmas.

I told Santa, my parents, the grandparents, the elves. I cut out trampoline pictures from catalogs and magazines and left them on counters and tabletops everywhere. I was sure I would get one. That morning I went running to see it. I looked out the window to the backyard where I expected it would be. But there, leaning against a tree, was a Pogo™ stick instead. I didn't even open the back door. Some surprises drop you and your expectations down into disappointment.

On the other hand, a surprise can come find you, be everything you hoped for, and bring joy to your world. For instance, years later, when I was married, my husband and I had to move. We were not able to afford Mayflower Van Lines, so we lined up our friends to help. The day or two before the move, surprise calls began to come in. He regretted he wouldn't be there because he got called in to work. She hated she wouldn't be able to make it because she was mistaken about the weekend. They were sorry they couldn't come; they had unexpected company.

So two of us began to work. We planned on packing all night. We had until noon the next day to hand the keys to a clean house over to the next tenants, who were practically camping out at the door. We tried to load all the furniture and appliances, but some were just too heavy. Our hands were sore from scrubbing fast and hard; but the spots were stubborn, and the house was growing larger by the minute. We were losing ground.

Some friends stopped by to pack a little and talk a lot, so when they left we still had more to do and less time to do it. In the lateness of the hour, full of worry, out of energy, and sinking down into despair, I sat down on the one kitchen stool we had left out and began to wonder what I should do. Helpless, I began to pray and started to cry.

Then I heard the back door open and shut. First heavy steps began coming my way. Then I heard his voice–kind, soft, and familiar. I never expected my father, but he was there. He came out of nowhere. He had driven for hours to get to us. He had strength and tools. He was tall, and he had a truck. He bought food and gave hugs. He would be there until the nasty job was finally done. He was the best surprise.

In Micah's day Jerusalem had some high hopes. Everyone said God was in Jerusalem granting the city perpetual beauty, love, joy, and peace. All the leaders and ministers of the day provided every assurance that it was so. God and peace ruled over Jerusalem. After all, Jerusalem was the city of God:

> where the waters flow gently down (Isa. 8:6);
> where God blessed King David, and King Solomon
>   built God's glorious temple;
> where strong walls stand and strong defenses keep
>   out all evil;
> where wars cease, be they fights against Assyria in
>   701 B.C.E. or against Babylon 114 years later.

Jerusalem, Zion, would never fail to be the place of God's grace and peace. The expectations were great. But Micah said not to look for God in Jerusalem. God was not there as much as sin was right then. Micah got specific and began to name the problems that took God away from that place. He made a list:

People talk about peace, but the hungry are not fed.
People are not kind or merciful.
People eat up each other in Jerusalem.
The rich are not sympathetic, and the strong press
  down hard on the weak.
The judges take bribes, and the preachers do not
  preach.
There is no justice, no mercy, no acts of kindness,
  and no care.
So there is no peace!

Micah said people would look for God and peace in Jerusalem one day, but neither would be found there anymore. He said God's anger might pour down on them like water off of a steep cliff, and God's fire might melt their mountain. Micah said Jerusalem might be plowed up one day and left in a heap of ruins.

Micah's prophecy can make you stop during Advent to see where you are and where you really want to be. He points to the holy place so we can turn around and go there if we know we need to find God and peace all over again. It is here:

You, O Bethlehem of Ephrathah,
  who are one of the little clans of Judah,
from you shall come forth for me one who is to
  rule...
    he shall be great
  to the ends of the earth;
and he shall be the one of peace.
  (5:2, 4b–5a)

Surprise! God will be in Bethlehem, Micah said. Peace will be born one day in Bethlehem. Look there. This was Micah's good news.

Bethlehem is not the place you would think to train one to lead you in anything. Kings would not select Bethlehem for their coronation ceremonies; Jerusalem would be the place for that. Jerusalem is where peacemakers and peace movements convene, not Bethlehem.

But Bethlehem is the place where Mary serves God at a cost—red eyes, cold hands, a dress stained from bearing a baby. Bethlehem is where Joseph is, face lined from worrying and moving against the wind. He is having disturbing dreams when he lies down, and he is not sure about tomorrow. Yet he is willing to hang there and to care at great lengths. Bethlehem is where a baby gets human love and a blanket.

God's peace will not be up on Jerusalem's hilltops where peace is declared but nothing is done to make it or to keep it. God's peace will be down in Bethlehem where peace is being bloody birthed, prayed for, and sung about as justice coming. Bethlehem is where peace will breathe little breaths, on and on, through this child, for Bethlehem, for Mary and Joseph, for lost Jerusalem, for the ends of the earth.

Micah never revealed this baby's name, but we call him Jesus. He was born there. He would grow up and call for justice. He would stand for mighty justice and bring it many times in the power of God. He would love Jerusalem and cry out to it long after Micah did, *"Would that even today you [that is, Jerusalem] knew the things that make for peace"* (Lk. 19:42, RSV). He would lead us to God and peace—small towns and great cities, nations, *the earth*.

People do long for peace. We want inner peace and peace all around us. We want justice so we can lie down and wake up in peace. Can that baby really bring us peace inside? Can that little child in Bethlehem truly make peace between us? Peace can be so hard to find, and God can be even harder. If we look in places like Bethlehem instead of Jerusalem, will we begin to know the way to peace?

I went to the mall on a Friday night, ten days before Christmas. The lines were long, and people were talking while they waited. "Have a Holly, Jolly Christmas" was playing in the background, and two women in front of me were huffing and puffing because of Christmas—the cost, the worry, the stolen peace, the feeling of being trapped by Christmas.

Micah 5:1–5a   123

They began to talk about what they would do the minute they got home. The young woman said first she would free her feet, then let her body rest in loose pajamas. She would cuddle herself up in her cozy chair, drink coffee latte in her large cup, read a book about the simple life, and let no one know where she was. She didn't want to deal with politics, or problems, or anything.

The older woman said her peace would cost fifty-five dollars and come tomorrow morning on the chiropractor's table. A man turned around and said he would find his Christmas peace out in the fields far away from crowds and women. He added that peace could be in New York if the stock market report was good.

I cannot imagine telling any of them Micah said to look for peace in Bethlehem.

Maybe if more than one star twinkled over that stable, I could suggest that they look there.

Maybe if I told them how peace from here was so powerful that it made the great King Herod shake in his royal shoes and run to Bethlehem to stop the kind of peace happening there.

Maybe if a movie star had sung the peace song there about this new day of God's justice and grace for a world of sin, instead of one young mother laying her baby down to sleep outside in the animal trough, not knowing *what* she would do the next night.

Who wants to go to a place like Bethlehem? Who expects to find peace there?

Telling people to go to Bethlehem to find God and peace is like telling people to become poor on purpose and see how it makes them rich. It is like telling people to go fill up the hungry with good things and see how full they will feel themselves, or for you to go give some money to shelter someone and see how warm you grow. It is like telling people to take on a burden and see how it can be light.

I am afraid many people will not go to Bethlehem for Christmas. Even if Micah tells them a Savior is born there, even if peace and goodwill are to be born there!

I was invited to dinner in Bethlehem. I had to decide whether to go or not. I had been there before, and I remembered the other guests at the table were two cats and a dog. The host served me one slice of white bread served on top of the peanut butter jar. The knife had been wiped off and handed to me so I could use it next. I remembered the good things at the table for me, too. Again I felt the kindness, gratitude, and love expressed in many little ways. I remembered how the pace was slow. I recalled that I left carrying away with me a deep peace and a sense that I had been near God. There I found something very human and very holy. I could decide not to go, though. I could go instead where I knew the food would be catered, everybody's nails would be manicured, and all the conversation would be pleasant. I had to decide where to go for Christmas.

One Saturday a young couple from our neighborhood was riding home in their sports utility vehicle with their three children: Maria, Shane, and the little one they called Maddie, short for Madison. The mother called to share with me what had happened to them. They had endured a long day. They attended a grand birthday party with lots of great presents. Their hosts provided generous party favors for everyone, rich food, and plenty of fun.

They had gone shopping after that. They had one more stop to make, by the nursing home to see great-grandmother, who had not seen the children in more than a year. After the visit, on the way home, it got so quiet in the car. Maybe it was the sickness or the nearness to death that caused it. Maybe it was the cold darkness and the newly falling snow.

The father felt something in the air and said quietly, "It's beginning to feel like Christmas." Then Maria, the eight-year-old daughter, said without a thought, "Yes. Now that we have been to see Grammie, it does." The parents looked at each other in such surprise at where the child had felt Christmas.

Certainly we can find plenty of ways to forget about Micah and stay far away from anything that even looks or smells like Bethlehem. We can avoid the long night and the weariness there, the pain and the fears there, the anxieties, the hard hopes and the tears there. Yes, all these appear in Bethlehem, and we can avoid them.

We can just pamper the pampered children some more. We can give to the ones who get all the time and never consider anyone or any place else. In fact, we can get lost and tired and cranky and bored in places just like Jerusalem and never have to get to the baby in Bethlehem and his justice or his peace at all.

Prayer

God, in this church, grant us freedom from our fears and power to follow Jesus Christ into God's peace for the world. Show us, each one, where Bethlehem is and help us to enter it, working for the justice and peace of God as Christ Jesus did. He is our peace. Amen.

CHAPTER 10

Micah 6:1–8

Exegesis

Here we have the suspense and drama of a courtroom scene. A courtroom has suspense because a decision must be made; it has drama because emotions run so high. Going to court represents a failure. People go to court because something has broken down. Someone has violated regulations or expectations, and attempts at negotiations have not succeeded.

A trial is often a last resort. This passage, then, represents God's deep feelings, and perhaps even a note of desperation. God sees no other recourse for recalcitrant Israel than bringing the people to trial. As we read this passage carefully, though, we will see that, in God's courtroom, unexpected things can happen.

Although the courtroom metaphor dominates this pericope, it really is a blend of different genres. Verses 1–5 explicitly picture a court scene and contain the Hebrew word for lawsuit (rib, v. 2). At verse 6, the language changes to liturgy. Verse 6 even sounds like a call to worship. Nevertheless, the final editing of this passage incorporates this liturgical language into the courtroom metaphor. This blending is consistent with the Old Testament view of life as unified. The sphere of worship was of one piece with the legal sphere. The final result might be outlined as follows.

vv. 1–2 Summons to court and seating of the jury.
vv. 3–5 YHWH's testimony.
vv. 6–7 An attempt at a plea bargain.
v. 8 The sentence.

When court is called into session, the roles are assigned. YHWH is the plaintiff; the prophet is the prosecuting attorney; the mountains, hills, and depths of the earth are the judge and jury; Israel is the defendant. The charge against Israel is that the people have violated the covenant that YHWH had established with them. The real evidence for this violation comes in chapters 1–3 of Micah. The people have not attended to justice, the needs of the poor, or the social fabric.

Up to the end of verse 2 of chapter 6, the courtroom scene fits our expectations, even if having the hills and mountains as the jury makes this a courtroom on a grand scale. At verse 3, however, the roles are reversed. YHWH, who has brought the lawsuit against Israel, begins to testify. YHWH's testimony, however, sounds like a defense. YHWH asks, in first person, "what have I done?" and "in what have I wearied you?" YHWH then recites the divine saving acts that formed Israel and established the covenant between Israel and YHWH. YHWH delivered the people from slavery in Egypt, provided Moses, Aaron, and Miriam (synecdoche for all of the prophets and leaders YHWH sent), and protected the people from foreign threats (using Balak and Balaam as synecdoche). YHWH's testimony establishes YHWH's innocence, even though Israel is the defendant.

YHWH's testimony indicates at least two things. First, if YHWH is innocent, then blame for the rupture in the relationship must belong to Israel. YHWH has kept up the divine side of the bargain. YHWH has created, protected, and supported the people of Israel.

Secondly, the tone of YHWH's testimony suggests a sense of hurt and pain. YHWH practically pleads with Israel in verse 3, "what have I done?" The verse sounds almost as though it comes not from a criminal trial, but from divorce proceedings. A heartbroken spouse might ask plaintively, "what have I done?" In this way, the passage reminds us of Hosea 11, where YHWH feels genuine pain at the broken relationship.

By verse 6, Israel, the defendant, seems convinced of their guilt. The question at this point is what the "penalty phase" of the trial will require. The attempts of the defendant to plea bargain begin with customary sacrifices (burnt offerings and calves a year old), move to the outlandish (thousands of rams), then to the absurd (ten thousands of rivers of oil), and end with the offensive (a firstborn child). The implication of the progression is that no sacrifice will satisfy the debt or restore the damaged relationship. The plea bargain is rejected.

The court then "sentences" the defendant to a renewed effort to live within the covenant. YHWH does not want the defendant punished so much as the relationship restored. The sentence is not punitive, but therapeutic. The court sentences Israel to "community service," with three requirements: "to do justice, and to love kindness, and to walk humbly with your God." That the "sentence" is not punitive indicates that God is not ultimately interested in punishment, but in restoration.

To do justice is to enact the elements of fairness in all aspects of society. Doing justice is work, observant and diligent work to identify and correct injustice. Loving kindness is perhaps the most unexpected part of the sentence. The expectation is not just that the defendant will perform the right actions, but also develop a genuine passion for showing kindness. The final requirement is that the defendant should walk humbly with God. The Hebrew word for "humbly" carries the connotation of wisely or prudently. One of the expectations of YHWH, the plaintiff, was that Israel should "know" what YHWH has done (v. 5). Walking humbly/wisely with God entails remembering God's grace and power, so that one lives in gratitude and devotion.

Sermon

"God's Courtroom"

We can't seem to get enough of TV shows, movies, or novels about what goes on in courtrooms. From *Perry Mason*, John Grisham, *Matlock, The Firm, The Practice, Judge Judy,* and *Ally McBeal,* courtrooms fill our entertainment lives. I read a few years ago that when *L. A. Law* was popular, applications to law schools went up. Phrases such as, "You can't handle the truth!"–snarled by Jack Nicholson to Tom Cruise in a military court in *A Few Good Men*–have worked their way into popular culture.

Maybe we find courtrooms so compelling because law cases are high drama. The whole atmosphere is tense and emotional. One side will win, and one side will lose. The judge and jury will try their best to dig out the truth. Important issues and principles are at stake. Large sums of money could change hands. How we understand our freedom and our responsibility could shift. What goes on in law courts is dramatic.

The drama of the courtroom came front and center a few years ago in real life in the O. J. Simpson trial. For almost a year, daytime TV was put on hold as much of the nation obsessed over this one trial. We were fascinated and repulsed at the same time. Networks hired analysts to explain to us what each bit of evidence meant. After months of testimony, the end finally came.

The way the verdict was announced could not have been more tense. On a Friday, the jury made its decision. Judge Lance Ito would not let the jury's finding be read until the next Monday. Over the long weekend, much of the country held its collective breath, because we really didn't know which way it would go. The experts disagreed, and the hours ticked by as we waited. When the verdict finally came, it was controversial, almost dividing the nation along racial lines. Such is the power of the courtroom. Whether fictional or real, it insists on our attention, because it carries power, authority, and the search for truth.

The prophet Micah portrays a courtroom drama. This is a courtroom like no other we have seen before. The courthouse is as big as all creation, with the mountains, hills, and depths of the earth seated as the jury. The Lord is the plaintiff. The prophet is the prosecuting attorney, and God's people are the defendants.

God's courtroom does not work like other courtrooms. In the passage itself, no charges are read against the defendant. Instead, God, the plaintiff, addresses the defendants directly. God's words sound part angry and part pleading. "O my people, what have I done to you? / In what have I wearied you? Answer me!" God seems to be asking, "Are you tired of having me as your God?" God is a very unusual plaintiff here. God doesn't seem to press the case of the people's guilt; God asks what is wrong with the relationship.

Although God doesn't say it directly, God's words imply that the people must be tired of having God around, because they aren't acting like the people of God. If charges have been filed against the people, they were filed earlier in the book. The people of God are on trial because the rich exploit the poor, taking their land away from them, driving widows and children out of their homes. The leaders of the people are no better than cannibals who tear the skin off of the backs of the poor, chewing them up and spitting them out.

The people are on trial, ironically, because their own law courts are corrupt, with justices taking bribes. The priests are hungry for money. The people of God are not living up to their end of the bargain.

In God's courtroom, the whole people are on trial, not just the individuals responsible for specific crimes. In God's courtroom, the people of Israel are expected to work together for the good of everyone. Everybody holds everyone else accountable. All of the people are responsible for the spiritual health of the whole community. The whole community is on trial.

God has the right to bring the community to trial because God formed them as a community. God took a band of slaves in Egypt, led them out of captivity, guided them through the wilderness, and formed them into a nation. God sent prophets and prophetesses among them to guide them and to lead them in celebration. Without God, they wouldn't be who they are. God thinks they have forgotten who they are, and so they are on trial.

The people of God offer no defense of their actions. They seem to admit their guilt implicitly. The trial moves to the sentencing phase, and the sentence is expressed in the language of worship. If the charge is that the people have not responded to God's love, then the sentence must be that the people worship more faithfully. So the defendant begins to plea bargain. The first offer is a normal amount of sacrifice: a burnt offering of year-old calves. The amount goes up with each line of the passage. If a burnt offering of year-old calves is not enough, how about thousands of rams? If thousands of rams are not enough, what about ten thousands of rivers of oil? The offering is approaching the ridiculous. The guilty defendant even wonders if the sacrifice of a first born child might be required.

God does not want the sentencing phase of the trial to be about an offering. Formal worship is fine and good, but it should not be an offering to appease God. Worship is the grateful response to God's forgiveness, as is our work for justice in society. In God's courtroom, the sentence is what no human judge could or would give. A human judge passes out specific sentences: so much time, so much money, so many hours of community service. But hear God's sentence: "Do justice." Do things that make the world fairer, more honest, more equal. Do a court system where people's rights are respected. Do an economy in which the homeless are taken care of. God doesn't say how much justice, only "do justice."

God's sentence continues with "Love kindness." A human judge can order us to do something, but only God can sentence us to love something. God sentences the defendant to love kindness. God's sentence is to fall in love with showing faithful and dependable kindness to others.

The final term of the sentence is the one we might have expected to come first–to walk humbly with God. Perhaps the other two came first to put the emphasis on doing justice and loving kindness. Doing justice and loving kindness are part of how we walk humbly with God. We can't have a healthy relationship with God if we don't care about other people.

Micah uses the drama of the courtroom to get the people's attention. God wants our attention as well. God has led us out of slavery to sin and formed us as the church. We know that if God were to put us on trial, Christ has paid any penalty we would owe. Nevertheless, because God has set us free from sin and death and formed us as the church, God expects us to do justice and to love kindness as part of our walk with God. In our individual lives, God wants us to do justice and to love kindness.

Beyond that, God wants us to be concerned about the whole community. Are people treated fairly and justly in our whole community? Two examples of injustice in Texas have come to light recently. Governor Bush, on the campaign trail for the office of President, said that he didn't believe any hungry people lived in Texas. Those who work directly with the poor in Texas say that, yes, lots of hungry people survive in Texas, even in the midst of good economic times. Micah would say that ignoring the poor and hungry is not justice. The problem is not just a governor's problem or a president's problem. We are all called to reach out to the hungry.

The second example is that scientists can now use DNA evidence to determine, in some cases, whether a person has committed a crime. Several times recently, DNA evidence has indicated that a person convicted of a crime did not commit the crime. Nevertheless, some prosecutors in Texas are not allowing these innocent people to go free. Micah would say that that is not justice.

God calls the church to speak out, even to cry out against injustice. God calls us to work diligently for justice. The church and the synagogue are the conscience of society and the government. We are the watchdogs guarding the territory of justice. God has a way of taking even the smallest of our efforts and blessing them, expanding them, working through them. God can use us to help others if we will do justice and fall in love with kindness.

SERMON

"The Minimum Daily Requirement"

Timothy K. Bruster

> Hear what the LORD says:
> Rise, plead your case before the mountains,
>   and let the hills hear your voice.
> Hear, you mountains, the controversy of the LORD,
>   and you enduring foundations of the earth;
> for the LORD has a controversy with his people,
>   and he will contend with Israel.
> "O my people, what have I done to you?
>   In what have I wearied you? Answer me!
> For I brought you up from the land of Egypt,
>   and redeemed you from the house of slavery;

and I sent before you Moses,
    Aaron, and Miriam.
O my people, remember now what King Balak of
    Moab devised,
  what Balaam son of Beor answered him,
and what happened from Shittim to Gilgal,
    that you may know the saving acts of the Lord."
"With what shall I come before the Lord,
    and bow myself before God on high?
Shall I come before him with burnt offerings,
    with calves a year old?
Will the Lord be pleased with thousands of rams,
    with ten thousands of rivers of oil?
Shall I give my firstborn for my transgression,
    the fruit of my body for the sin of my soul?"
He has told you, O mortal, what is good;
    and what does the Lord require of you
but to do justice, and to love kindness,
    and to walk humbly with your God?
(Micah 6:1–8)

The prophets in the Hebrew Scriptures were not simply fortune-tellers who foretold the future. Rather, they spoke the word of God to the situation in which they found themselves. Sometimes it involved what would happen in the future. Sometimes their words would rehearse what God had done in the past. Always their message spoke to what was going on in the lives of the people in relationship to God and to one another in the present.

The words of the prophets spoke not only to the people of their day and time, but they also speak to us today as we think about our own lives and what God is doing in our world and our relationship to God and to one another.

In this text we hear from the prophet Micah. In the sixth chapter he uses the image of a court of law. The courtroom is a vast valley, surrounded by mountains and hills. In this cosmic courtroom God brings a case against the people and says, "Rise, plead your case before the mountains, / and let the hills hear your voice." He says that the mountains, the hills, and the foundations of the earth are the witnesses and the jury. They have been around from the beginning, and they have seen it all. He says, "Hear, you mountains, the controversy of the LORD, / and you enduring foundations of the earth; / for the LORD has a controversy with his people, / and he will contend with Israel."

Then, the Lord asks, "O my people, what have I done to you? / In what have I wearied you? Answer me! / For I brought you up from the land of Egypt, / and redeemed you from the house of slavery; / and I sent before you Moses, Aaron, and Miriam." The Hebrew involves a little play on words that we can hear if we translate it, "Why are you *fed up* when I *brought you up* out of slavery in Egypt?" God then goes on to recount some of the wonderful and loving things that God has done for the people.

The painful thing for God, as God brings this case before the mountains and the hills, is that God cannot understand the response of the people. At best they are apathetic. At worst, they have turned away. They have sinned. They have hurt their neighbors. They have been uncaring. They have worshiped other gods—false idols they have set up. They have done evil.

The people's response in the courtroom is to offer a settlement! Listen to the words representing the people's side: "With what shall I come before the LORD, / and bow myself before God on high? / Shall I come before him with burnt offerings, / with calves a year old? / Will the LORD be pleased with thousands of rams, / with ten thousands of rivers of oil? / Shall I give my firstborn for my transgression, / the fruit of my body for the sin of my soul?"

This lone speaker, speaking on behalf of the people, uses more and more exaggerated suggestions of how he might make things right with God. Would a burnt offering do it? Calves a year old? Then the offer gets ridiculous suggesting extravagant gifts. How about thousands of rams given in offering? Or tens of thousands of rivers of oil given in offering? Finally, the people's representative makes a suggestion that would be strictly against the law of God—a suggestion that would be absolutely forbidden: What if I gave my firstborn, my child, as a sacrifice? You see, Israel did not practice human sacrifice as most of their neighbors did. God forbade it (Lev. 20:2). In desperation, the representative forgets logic and tries to express the most valuable things in life he can think of. What can I give on behalf of the people?

Then God provides the answer to the question. His decision differs drastically from the expected answer. You see, the suggestions that the speaker for the people gives are all about the ritual and the worship life of the people. What can we do in worship to make things right with God? What rituals can we perform? What offerings can we burn? What words can we speak?

Today, if we represented our church in God's courtroom, we might say something like, "What would make it up to you, O Lord? What if we said the right combination of prayers? What if we sang the right hymn? What would be the right response, God? What if we formed a committee? What if we passed the right resolution at our Church Conference? What if we read the Bible? What if we joined a discussion group? What if we set a goal of a million dollars for a special offering?"

There is nothing wrong with any of these things, just as nothing was wrong with the Israelite representative's answers—until he became desperate and proposed human sacrifice.

The real answer of how we can possibly respond to God is vastly different, but it is nothing new. The people to whom Micah prophesied had heard it before—and we've heard it before. Listen to this: "He has told you, O mortal, what is good" (Micah 6:8a). Notice that the prophet uses an unusual form of address: The *New Revised Standard Version* translates it, "O mortal." In the Hebrew, it is *'adam,* which means "human being." Why this unusual way of addressing these prophetic words? Because the term *'adam* includes *all* of humanity and therefore emphasizes that God's expectations apply to *all* people—even those outside Israel.

The prophet goes on to make it clear that the Lord doesn't require the rivers of oil, the thousands of rams, the burnt offerings—in other words, the worship life. Those expressions are only part of the response to God's grace. Amos is even more pointed in his prophetic word that the rituals of the people who are not living justly, who are not living righteously, are abhorrent to God (Amos 5:21-23). It's not just about worship, about words, about ritual. It's about living out the response to God's grace. It's about relationships with people and relationship with God.

So, what does the Lord require? What are the daily, ongoing requirements of life as a faithful person—a life that is lived in response to all that God has done? To use the language of the FDA, what is the "Minimum Daily Requirement" expected of all people?

In verse 8 Micah says three things: "What does the Lord require of you / but to do justice, and to love kindness, / and to walk humbly with your God?" (Micah 6:8b).

First, **"do justice."** Do justice. The prophet Amos would say, even more poetically, "let justice roll down like waters" (Amos 5:24). *DO* justice. If we are leading a life in response to God's goodness, then we will do justice each day.

Notice that justice is not something you talk about. It doesn't say *talk* justice.

It's not something we just think about; it doesn't say *think* justice.

It's not something we just wish for; it doesn't say *wish* justice.

It's not something we complain about the lack of; it doesn't say *complain* about justice.

Rather it says, *"DO* justice."

Justice is something we do because God is faithful and just. We are called to work for justice, for fairness, for equality for all people, particularly those who are weak, particularly those who are outcast, particularly those who are powerless and so often exploited by others.

If you look at Jesus' ministry, you will soon see that his ministry was about justice. His ministry so often targeted those who were most in need, those who were most out of the loop, those who had the least power. Jesus went to the tax collectors and the sinners, those who were the outcasts in his day.

Jesus characterized his ministry as fulfilling the words of Isaiah: "The Spirit of the Lord is upon me, / because he has anointed me / to bring good news to the poor. / He has sent me to proclaim release to the captives / and recovery of sight to the blind, / to let the oppressed go free, / to proclaim the year of the Lord's favor" (Lk. 4:18–19).

Our call is to do justice. If we are to respond to God's goodness by doing what the Lord requires, then we must do justice.

Second, he says, **"love kindness."** What does the Lord require? If we are leading a life in response to God's goodness, then we will love kindness. If we are walking in the Spirit, then our lives will bear the fruit of kindness. When you think about it, so much of the scripture is about simple kindness. And we downplay it a bit because it's just too simple. We want something a little more complicated, something a little more complex, maybe a little more intricate, certain hoops we need to jump through in order to do God's will. But Micah simply says, "love kindness."

Think about what that means. To love something is to place it in an important place in our lives. To love something is to pay attention to it and to live by it. Therefore, to love kindness means that we will certainly think about kindness, live it out in our lives, make it important, pay attention to it, and, above all, *do* acts of kindness.

Jesus, in speaking of the judgment, put it powerfully: Those who are judged to be righteous come before the Lord. And the Lord says, "I was hungry and you gave me food, I was thirsty and you gave me something to drink, I was a stranger and you welcomed me, I was naked and you gave me clothing, I was sick and you took care of me, I was in prison and you visited me" (Mt. 25:35-36). Those are just acts of kindness. Love kindness.

Finally, if we are to live a life in grateful response to all that God has done for us and for God's love, we will **"walk humbly with our God."** Now the key word is "walk." This third command, "walking humbly," uses an unusual verb form in the Hebrew. "To walk with" may best be understood as "to live with in communion." We are to be in relationship with God, walk alongside of God, follow God, allow God to be at the center of our living. All of those are ways of walking humbly with God.

If we bear the name "Christian," that's a requirement for the life of faith–that we walk with God; that we are in relationship with God; that we live in communion with God.

To walk humbly with God really means at least a couple of things.

First, it means to acknowledge that God is the source of everything. That's what humility is about here. We so often misunderstand Christian humility. We want to turn it into saying, "Oh, what a wretched worm I am," when that's not really humility. Humility is acknowledging before God and before one another who we really are and who God really is and what our relationship is. It means acknowledging our utter dependence on God. It means saying that there are no self-made people; there are only God-made people. The psalmist said, "Know that the LORD is God. / It is he that made us, and we are his; / we are his people, and the sheep of his pasture" (Ps. 100:3). To walk humbly with our God means acknowledging everything we have and all that we are come from God, who is our source.

One day Thomas Merton told a fellow monk, "If I make anything out of the fact that I am Thomas Merton, I am dead. And if you make anything out of the fact that you are in charge of the pig barn, you are dead. Quit keeping score altogether, and surrender yourself with all your sinfulness to God who sees neither the score nor the scorekeeper but only his child redeemed by Christ."[1] Walking humbly with God means knowing that we are all God's children redeemed by Christ.

Second, to walk humbly with God means to pray. It's not just about walking with God; it's about talking with God. Paul said, "Pray without ceasing" (1 Thess. 5:17). Walking with God and talking with God go hand in hand. Sometimes at night I take a walk. Rarely do I walk by myself. Sometimes my wife, Susan, goes; sometimes one of our daughters; sometimes several of us. On rare occasions we all get our schedules together and go. When we walk, sometimes we walk in silence. Sometimes one of us does most of the talking; sometimes another. The important thing is that we are not alone. We are in relationship. And being together makes all the difference.

I believe that about my—and your—relationship with God. Walking humbly with God means sometimes talking, sometimes listening and being silent. Always, it means not being alone. Always it means being in relationship with God. Being together makes all the difference.

What does the Lord require of us? What's the Minimum Daily Requirement? It's simple—though not always easy: "to **do justice**, and to **love kindness**, and to **walk humbly with your God**."

Sermon

"Check!"

Alyce M. McKenzie

I have a habit of making lists. As a new school year begins, I seem to be making lists of my lists. My favorite part is checking things off my lists. Call me compulsive, but sometimes if I'm feeling overwhelmed, I write down things I've already done, just so I can check them off. Don't tell me I'm the only one who does this!

Sometimes I have vivid dreams with a message. Do you ever feel you're more attentive when you're asleep than when you are awake? A few weeks ago I dreamed I was walking through a graveyard crowded with graves of varying sizes and shapes, looking for something, but not knowing what. Suddenly, in the midst of the graveyard, I spotted a brand new gravestone. It read as follows: "Alyce Mundi McKenzie, August 17, 1955–August 17, 2000."

On this grave were no words of commendation: "devoted wife and mother; beloved pastor and teacher…" Not a shred of scripture, not even a scrap of Shakespeare. No words at all. Just a big, freshly etched ✔! Micah, the small-town boy from Moresheth, was just the sort to sound a wakeup call to the wealthy elite of Jerusalem. Micah had the quality that graced those prophets in Israel whose prophecies were preserved and canonized. Micah was constantly checking out his context and God's contouring of that context. Micah was attentive to the right things.

I wouldn't be surprised if he carried a sketchpad and drew what he saw as he walked about. He sketches the procession of the elite lining up at the temple to offer their animals and their harvest fruits, all decently and in good order.

He sketches the hopeless eyes of the vulnerable in this ancient episode of *Survivor,* in which the rich vote the poor out of their houses and take their few possessions. Why? because they can!

I picture Micah sitting in the front row as the local preacher stands up to begin his message: sketching the speaker's unctuous expression. "This morning's sermon, like last week's, is entitled, 'Whatever you are already doing is God's will.' Today we answer the question that burns within each one of us: 'What does the good life require?' The answer: 'to assure our personal security, to minimize our responsibility to others, and to walk in the way of prosperity!'"

As his sketchpad fills up with these sights and sounds, Micah is constantly checking in with God. His very name means, "Who is like Yahweh?" In chapter 6, verses 1–5, Micah sketches a courtroom scene. He's not sketching Judge Wapner and two people haggling over a toaster oven. He's sketching God drawing near to criticize Israel and offer a recital of God's mighty acts.

As God and Israel come out of the courtroom and into the hall, it's unlike any television courtroom show you've ever seen. On television, everybody always feels they should have won, and nobody who wins ever feels they got enough. But here the people say, "We were wrong. Now, what can we offer you, God, as we come into your presence?"

On Tuesday night, I enjoyed attending the student talent show after our annual fall banquet. The highlight of the talent show was a game show spoof called, "Who wants to be a seminarian?" It featured multiple-choice questions like, "Where was John Wesley's heart strangely warmed?" a. Oxford b. Georgia c. Aldersgate d. Taco Cabana. The multiple-choice question with which our text begins would almost qualify as a question for a humorous game show spoof:

> "Which of the following is the gift we can bring into
>   God's presence to meet God's requirements and
>   gain divine forgiveness?"
> Burnt offerings?
> Calves a year old?

Thousands of rams?
Ten thousands of rivers of oil?
My firstborn for my transgressions?
(Micah 6:6, 7 paraphrased)

This doesn't work as humor, though, because it's not funny. We can hear too clearly the escalating desperation of the answers, and they are all the wrong answers.

Students—new and returning—faculty, and staff, with what do you come before the Lord this first day of classes of the academic year 2000–2001 at Perkins School of Theology?

Before our lists of things to do get any longer, now is the moment to check and see...

Look, God, I've brought a full day-timer.
I've brought a sense of grim duty.
I've brought guilt and the inability to say no.
I've brought a racing mind.
I've brought a troubled heart.

What God wants, according to the prophet, is our attention. The Hebrew behind the phrase "to walk humbly with your God" is more accurately rendered "to walk attentively" with God. We know how to walk attentively: to the criticism of others, to our own inward anxieties, to the seduction of a radically individualistic, acquisitive culture.

Can we walk attentively with regard to God, checking what God is doing in our lives?

Can we be attentive to the grace in the grind?

Can we be attentive to the struggling colleague whose pain we sense?

Can we view our studies, not as hoops to jump through, but venues for the grace of God through Jesus Christ?

Can we be attentive to God?

Well, yes, of course we can, or we wouldn't even be here!

Well, no, of course we can't, given all the things we have to do this semester!

God help us! How we need to be attentive to God for one another's sake, not to mention the church and the world! How we need the communal graces that flow from walking attentively with God. How we need to love mercy—that is, to love ourselves and one another looking to the way God loves God's people. Loving mercy means being attentive to where it is lacking.

Here it pays to be attentive to the children. "Mommy, that man's sign says he's hungry and has no home. Can we take him home with us and feed him?"

"Mom, why do they kill so many people here in Texas? Can they be sure everybody was really guilty?"

How we need the communal graces that flow from walking attentively with God! How we need to do justice! How we need to care for the vulnerable in our midst, looking to the way God desires justice for the widow as well as wise man, for the orphan as well as the chief priest.

Let's check the syllabus before we go any further in the course. What does the Lord require of us? The Lord requires that the condition of the helpless and the poor, the struggling and the lonely, make a claim on our passion, our conduct, and our attention! Even while we're in seminary!

Some years ago a family moved into a community. At least one person in the community did not feel they belonged there. Words were spray painted on their home and sidewalk. Their tires were slashed. Driving by the house on his way to church one morning, the pastor of the community church saw all this. He turned his car around and drove back home. He got a lawn chair and a jug of lemonade. He went and sat down in their front yard—all that day; all that night. He woke up there early the next morning just in time to see somebody passing by. He was surprised by who it was. "Hey, you're up early. Got your spray paint I see. Oh, you're touching up your car? Drive on by, and let me see how it comes out when you're done. You have a good day."

He kept sitting there, doing nothing, except justice. A couple of others came and sat with him. I wish I could say hundreds—that might make a better story—or maybe not. Maybe it's a good enough story that in this case, just a couple of people was all it took.

When we walk attentively with God, we love mercy and do justice. We also nurture the habit that can sustain us in the traumatic times that an unpredictable life may hold.

When my mother was in the hospital having my younger sister, she had a difficult labor and delivery. My sister was underweight, but able to breathe on her own. She was sleeping in the nursery down the hall.

My mother had overheard the nurses talking about her roommate's situation. This young mother had also had a hard labor. She had come out of it all right, but her baby was still struggling in the neonatal intensive care unit. After overhearing that conversation, my mother fell into a much-needed sleep. She woke up early in the morning still groggy from painkillers. Turning her head, she noticed her roommate lying in the next bed. Her eyes were closed. Her face was pale. But she was moving her lips, saying something with such surety that my mother could read her lips even from across the room. She was saying, "This is the day the Lord has made. I will rejoice and be glad in it. This is the day the Lord has made. I will rejoice and be glad in it. This is the day the Lord has made. I will rejoice and be glad in it."

She opened her eyes and noticed my mother looking at her. Summoning the best smile she could, she asked, "Why should today be any different from any other day?"

My brothers and sisters in Christ, we can live this semester checking things off our lists, or we can live this semester checking in with God. Amen!

NOTES

Introduction: What Is a Prophetic Preacher?

¹I presented some of the ideas in this chapter to a meeting of the Academy of Homiletics at Dallas, Texas, in December of 2000. At that meeting, I suggested that all preaching can be prophetic preaching because all preaching can draw upon the prophets. A Roman Catholic priest from Poland, Father Henryk Slawinski, responded that not all preaching is prophetic preaching, but that "all *good* preaching is prophetic preaching."

²Ernest T. Campbell, "An Open Letter to Billy Graham," in *The Riverside Preachers,* ed. Paul H. Sherry (New York: The Pilgrim Press, 1978), 125–31.

³Campbell's words were, "The President needs a Micaiah not a Zedekiah, a prophet, not a mere house chaplain." (Sherry, 127). Campbell quotes Andersen, who at the time was pastor of First Presbyterian Church of LaGrange, Illinois, "I beg you to raise your voice as a prophet, like Nathan of old, in protest to the President, imploring him to stop the bombing [of North Vietnam] immediately" (ibid., 126).

⁴See John Bright, *A History of Israel* (Philadelphia: Westminster Press, 1981), 260: "Israelite society, as Amos lets us see it, was marked by egregious injustices and a shocking contrast between extremes of wealth and poverty. The small farmer, whose economic status was marginal at best, found himself often at the mercy of the moneylender and, at the slightest calamity–a drought, a crop failure–liable to foreclosure and eviction, if not bond service. The system, which itself was harsh, was made harsher by the greed of the wealthy, who took unmerciful advantage of the plight of the poor in order to enlarge their holdings, often resorting to the sharpest practices, the falsification of weights and measures and various legal dodges to achieve their ends."

⁵For more information on Baal, see John Day, "Baal," in the *Anchor Bible Dictionary,* ed. David Noel Freedman, et al. Volume 1 (New York: Doubleday, 1992), 545–49.

⁶Fred Craddock, *Preaching* (Nashville: Abingdon Press, 1985), 26. Emphasis in original.

Chapter 1: Introduction to Hosea

¹At least one commentator on Hosea believes that he was not a reformer, but a spiritual innovator, whose contribution to the history of Israel's religion was the insistence on exclusive worship of YHWH. See Gale A. Yee, "Hosea," in *The New Interpreter's Bible,* ed. Leander E. Keck and David L. Petersen, et al., vol. 7 (Nashville: Abingdon Press, 1996), 195–297, see especially pages 200–203.

²On the redaction of Hosea, see Yee, 200–206, and James L. Mays, *Hosea,* The Old Testament Library (Philadelphia: The Westminster Press, 1969), 15–17.

³In Renita Weems, *Battered Love: Marriage, Sex, and Violence in the Hebrew Prophets* (Minneapolis: Fortress Press, 1995), Weems explores carefully the marriage metaphor in the prophets. Although she acknowledges its problems, she sees it as a metaphor with great potential. "If we are willing, however, to sever the ties within the metaphor between the erotic and violence, between love and aggression, then the marriage metaphor might have the potential to shed light on a range of otherwise unexamined aspects of bonded love. We have seen elsewhere how the metaphor calls attention to the contractual character of the divine-human relationship, the stormy character of that relationship, the magnitude of the deity's love, the interrelatedness of life, and the fickleness of the human heart" (112).

⁴For a good, clear, brief treatment of these terms, see Bruce C. Birch, *Hosea, Joel and Amos* (Louisville: Westminster John Knox Press, 1997), 37.

⁵At issue is whether the woman in chapter 3 is still Gomer or another woman. See ibid., 40, for a brief discussion.

⁶In the courtroom metaphor, YHWH often changes roles, being at times the prosecuting attorney, a witness, and a judge. According to Ms. Versel Rush, an attorney in my current congregation, the words of YHWH at the beginning of Hosea 4 sound like the testimony of a victim.

⁷The Hebrew term here, *hesed,* is a rich and complex term. It is often used of God's love, which is constant and forgiving. James L. Mays says of its usage in this verse, "*Hesed* means the attitude and acts which loyally maintain and implement a given relationship, the covenant in Hosea's usage," (*Hosea,* 98).

⁸Birch comments, "To 'know God' has both a content and a commitment. Knowledge of God is related to torah, or instruction, and is the special responsibility of the priest (4:6). It is in this respect related to Israel's memory of what God has done and the relationship that has been established between God and Israel. But the Hebrew words for knowing and knowledge imply more than a content. They imply an acknowledgement and participation in relationship," (*Hosea, Joel, Amos,* 47).

Chapter 2: Hosea 2:14–23

¹See Gale Yee's treatment of the implications of this text in contemporary situations of spousal abuse. She concludes that the text should be used as a teachable moment to discuss domestic violence. ("Introduction, Reflections, and Commentary on the Book of Hosea," in *New Interpreter's Bible,* vol. 7 [Nashville: Abingdon Press, 1996], 226–29).

²James L. Mays, *Hosea,* Old Testament Library (Philadelphia: The Westminster Press, 1969), 9.

³Gale A. Yee, "Hosea," in *The Women's Bible Commentary,* ed. Carol A. Newsom and Sharon H. Ringe (London: SPCK and Louisville: Westminster/John Knox Press, 1992), 195.

Chapter 3: Hosea 11:1–11

¹Several explanations have been offered about why the Hebrew text of Hosea is so hard to understand. The two most likely are (1) that in the turmoil of the eighth century, the text was not copied well, and we have a damaged manuscript, or (2) that Hosea used a northern dialect of Hebrew, which we do not understand as well as the more well-represented southern dialect of most of the rest of the Hebrew Bible.

²Francis I. Andersen and David Noel Freedman, *Hosea: A New Translation with Introduction and Commentary,* Anchor Bible, ed. William Foxwell Albright and David Noel Freedman, no. 24 (New York: Doubleday, 1980), 574.

³See also James Luther Mays, *Hosea,* Old Testament Library (Philadelphia: Westminster Press, 1969), 154–55.

⁴See Douglas Stuart, *Hosea-Jonah,* Word Biblical Commentary, ed. David A Hubbard, et al., no. 31 (Waco, Tex.: Word Books, 1987), 175–76.

⁵Hosea uses a plural form here, perhaps indicating several gods. See Judges 2:11.

⁶It can also be a common noun, meaning "master," or "husband."

⁷See Joseph Blenkinsopp, *A History of Prophecy in Israel,* rev. and enlarged (Louisville: Westminster John Knox Press, 1996), 65–66.

⁸Preachers in other contexts, especially Eastern Europe, Africa, Latin America, and parts of Asia and the Middle East could speak directly to situations of political turmoil, destruction, and chaos that would be very similar to what Hosea's hearers experienced.

⁹James M. Ward, *Hosea: A Theological Commentary* (New York: Harper & Row, 1966), 197.

¹⁰James M. Ward, *Thus Says the Lord: The Message of the Prophets* (Nashville: Abingdon Press, 1991), 227.

¹¹Translation in Mays, *Hosea,* 150–51.

[12]Ward, *Thus Says the Lord,* 230.
[13]Philip D. Kenneson, *Life on the Vine: Cultivating the Fruit of the Spirit in Christian Community* (Downers Grove, Ill.: InterVarsity Press, 1999), 184.
[14]Ibid., 185, 190.
[15]Ibid., 191.
[16]Peter J. Gomes, *Sermons: Biblical Wisdom for Daily Living* (New York: Avon, 1998), 178–79.

Chapter 4: Introduction to Amos

[1]That Israel prospered under Jeroboam II, mentioned above in the chapter on Hosea, is a common assumption in Old Testament history. Some researchers point out, however, that our evidence for this prosperity is meager. At least in the minds of both Hosea and Amos, Israel enjoyed a time of economic expansion. See Keith W. Whitelam, "Jeroboam," in *The Anchor Bible Dictionary,* ed. David Noel Freedman, et al., vol. 3 (New York: Doubleday, 1992), 745–46.
[2]See Joseph Blenkinsopp, *A History of Prophecy in Israel,* rev. ed. (Louisville: Westminster John Knox Press, 1996), 73–74.
[3]See Robert B. Coote, *Amos Among the Prophets: Composition and Theology* (Philadelphia: Fortress Press, 1981). Other scholars disagree with this general conclusion. For a defense of the proposition that most, if not all, of the book derives from Amos himself, see Francis I. Andersen and David Noel Freedman, *Amos: A New Translation with Introduction and Commentary,* Anchor Bible 24A (New York: Doubleday, 1989), especially 141–44.
[4]See Blenkinsopp, *History of Prophecy,* 79.
[5]As Bruce C. Birch points out, "How easy it is to take delight in the judgment of others. We can be horrified at reports of violence elsewhere in the world but reluctant to admit anything is wrong in a society with more shootings and violent crimes per capita than any other nation in the world. We demand that courts and governments get tough on crime, especially in the inner city, but we often refuse to support taxes or laws that enable us to address the causes of crime. We will accept almost any responsibility for violence assigned to 'them' but resist the notion that any responsibility lies with 'us.' No doubt Amos would shock us too by suggesting that we can find ourselves judged along with others who have opposed God's will for justice and righteousness." *Hosea, Joel and Amos* (Louisville: Westminster John Knox Press, 1997), 185.
[6]Ibid., 186.
[7]I am grateful to Mrs. Lisa Bell, a member of First United Methodist Church in Bowie, Texas, for this quote.
[8]See James Limburg, *Hosea-Micah,* Interpretation (Atlanta: John Knox Press, 1988), 107.
[9]See Andersen and Freedman, *Amos: A New Translation,* 754–762.
[10]As James M. Ward points out, "What we learn from Amos's oracles is that poor and powerless people in Israel were being cheated, exploited, and denied justice in the courts by people wealthier and more powerful than they–people ridiculed by the prophet for their self-indulgent greed and self-serving religiosity. We also learn that such behavior was denounced as a violation of the will of God." From *Thus Says the Lord: The Message of the Prophets* (Nashville: Abingdon Press, 1991), 205.

Chapter 6: Amos 7:10–17

[1]See James L. Mays, *Amos,* Old Testament Library (Philadelphia: Westminster Press, 1969), 135.
[2]"Letter from Birmingham City Jail," in *A Testament of Hope,* ed. James M. Washington (San Francisco: Harper, 1986), 289–302. Particularly pertinent is the following quote, "I am in Birmingham because injustice is here. Just as the eighth century prophets left their little villages and carried their 'thus saith the Lord' far beyond the boundaries of their hometowns; and just as the Apostle Paul left his little

village of Tarsus and carried the gospel of Jesus Christ to practically every hamlet and city of the Graeco-Roman world, I too am compelled to carry the gospel of freedom beyond my particular hometown" (290).

[3] Joerg Rieger, ed., *Liberating the Future: God, Mammon and Theology* (Minneapolis: Fortress Press, 1998), 124–41.

Chapter 7: Introduction to Micah

[1] See Jeremiah 26, especially vv. 16–19.

[2] Some commentators divide the book into three sections, 1–2, 3–5, 6–7; others divide it into two sections, 1–5 and 6–7. See Ralph L. Smith, *Micah-Malachi* (Waco, Tex.: Word Books, 1984), 6–8 for a discussion of the ways Micah has been divided.

[3] Although Smith acknowledges that the book has been edited, he declares, "I believe that the prophet Micah furnished the inspiration for the entire project. The materials may have been edited and supplemented in the time of Jeremiah and again in the exilic or early post-exilic period by the prophetic disciples of Isaiah and Micah. But the basis for the entire book is found in the life and teachings of the prophet Micah and so dates back to his lifetime–about 700 B.C." (ibid., 8–9). Delbert R. Hillers, *Micah*, Hermeneia (Philadelphia: Fortress Press, 1984), 89 believes that part of chapter 7 could derive from Micah. For a defense of the position taken here, see James Luther Mays, *Micah*, Old Testament Library (Philadelphia: Westminster Press, 1976), 12–15.

[4] See, for example, James M. Ward, *Thus Says the Lord: The Message of the Prophets* (Nashville: Abingdon Press, 1991), 233.

[5] Samuel D. Proctor makes similar allegations against contemporary preachers, especially in the African American community, in his chapter "Prophetic Preaching Now: A Generation After King," in *Preaching on the Brink: The Future of Homiletics: In Honor of Henry H. Mitchell*, ed. Martha J. Simmons (Nashville: Abingdon Press, 1996), 156. "[S]adly, too many of our preachers are not calling our people to discipline and devotion. They are preaching a soft message of materialism and selfish regard. Services are dominated by the theme of what God gives us, not what we give in service and devotion."

[6] See *The Progressive Populist: A Monthly Journal of the Heartland* 4.8 (August 1998) for articles on the farm crisis in the United States. The crisis includes loss of land, income, and political indifference. Micah had a special concern for small farmers who could not protect themselves against powerful business leaders and politicians.

[7] In my Texas congregation, I suggested that we can visualize God as a giant cowboy boot, squashing a scorpion.

[8] The passage in its final form also mentions Israel, but that is likely a later gloss.

[9] The ideas of vulnerability and restoration appear in both books. God is vulnerable in Micah 6:3, and God restores in Hosea 14. Nevertheless, the book of Micah emphasizes restoration, and the book of Hosea emphasizes vulnerability.

[10] The article "A Living Wage," in *Christian Century* 118, no. 17 (May 23–30, 2001): 5–6, discusses some of the "top-down" issues, such as adequate wages for the working poor. Ronald Sider exemplifies those writers who speak to both sides of the issue. In a newspaper article, Sider praises President George W. Bush for his work on the "bottom-up" aspect of poverty, but chastises him for his neglect of the "top-down" aspects. In Sider's words, "Millions of Americans work full time and fail to earn enough to reach the poverty level. About 40 percent of all black and Latino single moms work full time without escaping poverty. Tens of millions can't afford health insurance. If compassionate conservatives won't use significant amounts of a huge budget surplus to correct these problems, when will they act?" ("Bush Must Address Other Half of Poverty," *Dallas Morning News*, 26 May 2001, 27A.)

Chapter 8: Micah 4:1–7

[1] Anna Quindlen, "Our Tired, Our Poor, Our Kids," *Newsweek* 137, no. 11 (March 12, 2001): 80.

²David France, "Slavery's New Face," *Newsweek* 137, no. 25 (December 18, 2000): 61.
³Versel Rush, "New Low: Actions of Dallas, Houston attorneys beg the question, 'Is Justice for Sale in Texas?'" *Wichita Falls Times Record News,* 25 February 2001, 2B.
⁴David Broder, "Book Reveals Death Row's Broken System," *Dallas Morning News,* 20 June 2000, 11A.

Chapter 9: Micah 5:1–5a

¹The English versification does not match the Hebrew. Verse 1 in English is 4:14 in Hebrew.
²James Luther Mays, *Micah,* Old Testament Library (Philadelphia: Westminster Press, 1976), 112–14.
³Delbert Hillers, however, considers verse 1 to be an isolated fragment. This seems unlikely, because an editor would have no reason to leave this verse hanging. Moreover, verse 1 explains why the new ruler is needed: The people are under siege. *Micah,* Hermeneia (Philadelphia: Fortress Press, 1984), 62–63.
⁴Mays, 111, 114; Ralph L. Smith, *Micah-Malachi,* Word Biblical Commentary (Waco, Tex.: Word Books, 1984), 42–43. Tanak refers to *The TANAKH, a new translation of the Holy Scriptures according to the traditional Hebrew text,* copyright © 1985 by the Jewish Publication Society; HCSB is the *Holman Christian Standard Bible®*, Copyright © 1999, 2000, 2002, 2003 by Holman Bible Publishers; NET refers to the *Holy Bible: The NET BIBLE® (New English Translation™),* copyright© 2001 by Biblical Studies Press, L.L.C. www.netbible.com available online at www.bible.org.
⁵NRSV refers to the *New Revised Standard Version Bible,* copyright 1989, Division of Christian Education of the National Council of the Churches of Christ in the United States of America; New Jerusalem to *The New Jerusalem Bible,* copyright 1985 by Darton, Longman & Todd, Ltd., and Doubleday, a division of Bantam Doubleday Dell Publishing Group, Inc.; REB to *The Revised English Bible,* copyright © Oxford University Press and Cambridge University Press, 1989; God's Word to *GOD'S WORD®*, a copyrighted work of *God's Word to the Nations,* 1995; NAB to the *New American Bible with Revised Psalms and Revised New Testament,* copyright © 1986, 1991 by the Confraternity of Christian Doctrine, 3211 Fourth Street, N.E., Washington, D.C. 20017.
⁶NIV refers to the HOLY BIBLE, NEW INTERNATIONAL VERSION®. NIV®, copyright © 1973, 1978, 1984 by International Bible Society; NLT to the *Holy Bible,* New Living Translation, copyright © 1996, Tyndale House Publishers, Inc., Wheaton, Illinois; NASB to the *NEW AMERICAN STANDARD BIBLE®*, © Copyright The Lockman Foundation 1960, 1962, 1963, 1968, 1971, 1972, 1973, 1975, 1977, 1995; ESV to *The Holy Bible, English Standard Version,* ©Crossway Bibles, 2004; NKJV to the *New King James Version,* copyright © 1979, 1980, 1982 by Thomas Nelson, Inc.; TEV to *Today's English Version*–Second Edition © 1992 by American Bible Society.
⁷Mays, *Micah,* 116–17, considers the phrase to be a metaphor for the time of the exile.
⁸ *TANAKH, a new translation of the Holy Scriptures according to the traditional Hebrew text,* (Philadelphia: The Jewish Publication Society, 1985). The Holman Christian Standard Bible and the NET Bible also translate in this way.
⁹This is derived not from the Hebrew text but from the Septuagint, the earliest Greek translation, and is followed by The New Jerusalem Bible, the Revised English Bible, and the New American Bible.
¹⁰Other translations following this option include New Living Translation, New American Standard Bible, English Standard Version, *God's Word,* and Today's English Version.

Chapter 10: Micah 6:1–8

¹*Homiletics* (January-February 1999): 44.

www.ingramcontent.com/pod-product-compliance
Lightning Source LLC
LaVergne TN
LVHW051603070426
835507LV00021B/2733